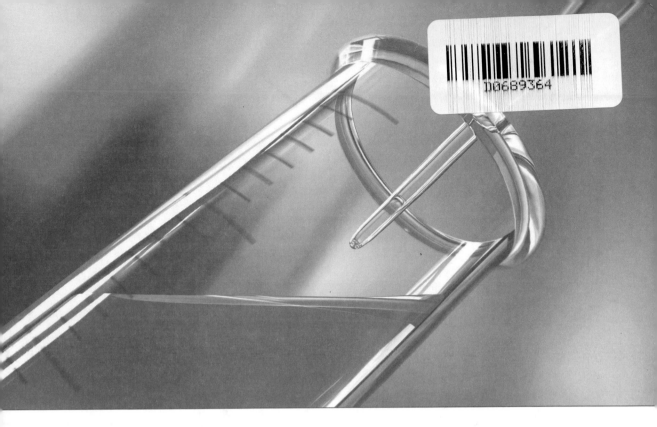

LABORATORY TECHNIQUES FOR GENERAL CHEMISTRY

Fourth Edition
Steven L. Brown

HAYDEN HM McNEIL

ISBN 978-0-7380-4472-9

Hayden-McNeil Publishing
14903 Pilot Drive
Plymouth, MI 48170
www.hmpublishing.com

Brown 4472-9 F11 V2

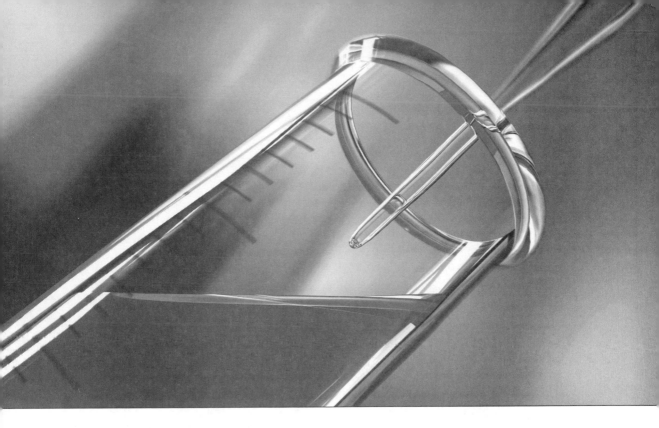

TABLE OF CONTENTS

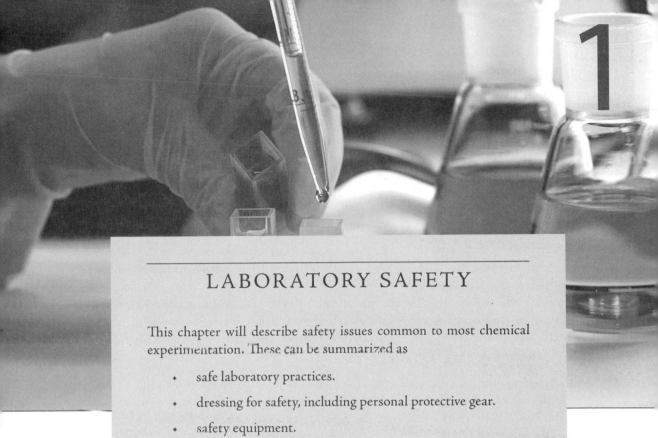

LABORATORY SAFETY

This chapter will describe safety issues common to most chemical experimentation. These can be summarized as

- safe laboratory practices.

- dressing for safety, including personal protective gear.

- safety equipment.

- handling chemicals.

- dealing with the unexpected.

- waste disposal.

By its nature the chemical laboratory can be a dangerous place to work. The improper use of chemicals and equipment can cause severe and/or permanent damage to your body. And you are not the only one at risk. Your actions can affect your coworkers, those who follow, and the environment. One of the more important aspects of your chemistry lab experience will be learning how to perform experiments as safely as is humanly possible. You will learn how to protect yourself and others from the hazardous conditions created by your experimentation.

This chapter covers general safety issues. Additional safety information will be presented with each experiment. Prior to each experiment your instructor will describe the proper use of chemicals and equipment. It is expected that you will become familiar with all this information. Your grade will depend, in part, on how well you demonstrate safe lab habits and knowledge of safe laboratory practices. You should expect to see the material presented here on the exams you take. In addition, your instructor's evaluation of your lab performance will be based, in part, on your adherence to safe laboratory practices and the lab rules. Finally, should you demonstrate a lack of regard for safety rules, or laboratory safety in general, you will be prohibited from working in the lab.

1-1 SAFE LABORATORY PRACTICES

It is common knowledge that doing chemistry is a hazardous activity. But so are cooking and driving a car. As with these other activities, the trick to a safe chemistry lab experience is to learn safe practices and develop safe working **habits**. This course is designed to teach safe lab practices and to help you develop habits that will lead to efficient, effective, and **safe** experimentation.

When performed correctly, the experiments presented in this course are safe. But this is a teaching lab. Mistakes will be made. Misinterpretation of the instructions or use of the wrong chemicals can result in a serious accident. And no matter how careful you are, the student working next to you may be doing something to endanger your health that you are helpless to prevent. No matter how much faith you have in your ability to work safely in the laboratory it is foolish to believe that an accident can't happen to you.

The safety rules are designed with this idea in mind. If you faithfully adhere to these rules, and to your instructor's precautions, you will find working in the chemical laboratory to be no more dangerous than working in a kitchen or driving a car.

Keep in mind that safety rules don't exist just to protect you and your lab mates. They are also intended to help instill safe working habits. Because habits are developed by repetition, it is expected that you will adhere to these rules at all times, regardless of the level of danger posed by any particular experiment.

An important component of a safe lab is cleanliness. A cluttered lab is a breeding ground for accidents. While performing an experiment, your work space should contain only those items that are currently needed. Spills should be immediately cleaned up. You must be aware at all times of the contents of all containers. At the end of the class you must turn off all water and gas jets, return all borrowed items and return all of your equipment to its proper storage location. You also must leave a clean workbench for the student that follows.

1-2 DRESSING FOR SAFETY

There are two dangers from chemical contact with skin:
1.   destruction of tissue (chemical burns) and
2.   poisoning due to absorption through the skin.

You should think about the materials you will wear to lab. Many fabrics, such as nylon and polyester, react with common lab chemicals. Most burn well. Cotton is the safest material to wear in a lab.

Clothing should be simple and loose fitting, but not too loose. You don't want to restrict your freedom of motion. Conversely, you don't want to accidentally dip a baggy sleeve into concentrated acid.

Lab Coat

To protect yourself against splashed chemicals and fumes, you should cover as much of your skin as is practical. A **lab coat** is ideal. Long pants are also highly recommended.

The selection of a lab coat should take into account the anticipated dangers of the lab. An appropriate lab coat will fit well—not too big or too small. The sleeves will be long enough to cover the arms, but not so long they get in the way. It will cover to below the knees.

Lab coats made of synthetic fabrics should NOT be used if there is a significant danger of fire. Synthetic fibers not only burn well but also melt and can stick to the skin. The best material for lab coats and all other clothing worn in a chemistry lab is cotton.

Once exposed to dangerous chemicals, a lab coat should be either properly cleaned or safely discarded.

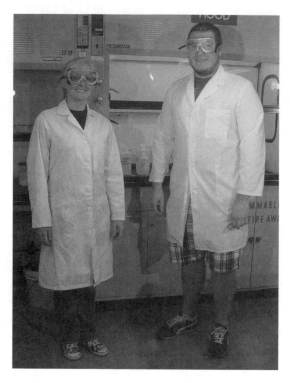

Figure 1-1. Lab coat.

Shoes

Because broken glass and spilled chemicals are common in the lab, nonabsorbent shoes that cover the entire foot are a must. Consider what would happen if you were wearing canvas sneakers and spilled acid on your shoe. It would soak through the shoe to your foot. In the time it would take you to get the shoe off, significant damage could be done. And it would be even worse if you were wearing socks.

©Hayden-McNeil, LLC

Figure 1-2. Acceptable footwear.

©Hayden-McNeil, LLC

Figure 1-3. Unacceptable footwear.

Gloves

 Hands present a special case. We use our hands to manipulate lab equipment and reagent bottles. This creates a large potential for inadvertent contact with chemicals, possibly resulting in chemical burns. *You will be instructed to wear gloves when you will be working with sufficiently dangerous chemicals.* The procedures in this lab manual that require the use of gloves are indicated with the glove icon.

Not all gloves are suitable for use in a lab. The ones you select must not interfere with your ability to manipulate delicate glassware and instruments. They must also be impermeable to water and solvents. And they must be comfortable. The best choice for most lab situations are nitrile examination gloves (see Figure 1-4).

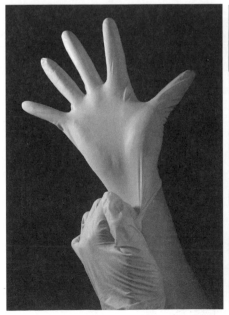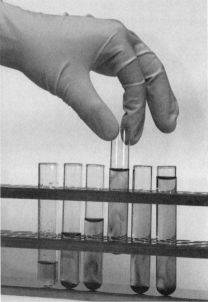

Figure 1-4. Lab gloves.

Eye Protection

Your eyes are quite possibly the most fragile parts of your body. They are certainly very important and impossible to replace. And they face many dangers in a chemical lab. *Proper protection of the eyes is mandatory in a chemical lab.*

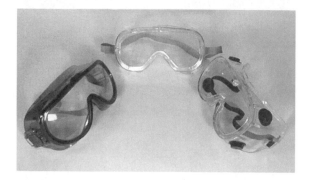

Figure 1-5. Vented goggles.

While explosions pose the most dramatic danger to your eyes, they are not very common in chemistry labs. The greatest danger is from splashed chemicals. **Safety glasses** provide protection against particles propelled toward you (e.g., as the result of an explosion), but are not effective against splashes. Goggles with perforations are better, but still not adequate in many situations. Only **vented goggles** are considered adequate to properly protect you from splashed chemicals and flying particles.

1-3 LABORATORY SAFETY EQUIPMENT

Safety Showers

These provide first aid should you come into contact with large amounts of a dangerous chemical. You need to know the location and proper operation of the safety showers in your lab. To use the shower, stand under the head and pull the chain. Continue the washing for 15 minutes. Some showers are designed to dump a certain amount of water before they shut off.

Figure 1-6. A lab safety shower.

Eyewash Stations

These provide first aid in the event some foreign body or chemical enters the eye. You need to know the location and proper operation of the nearest eyewash station to your work space. Should you get a chemical in your eye, or should chemical vapors cause your eyes to water, immediately wash your eyes with lots of water. To be effective, eyewashing must be continuous for at least 15 minutes.

Figure 1-7. Eyewash fountain.

Fume Hoods

These are designed to prevent dangerous fumes, gasses, and vapors from entering the lab. They require a certain face velocity and are normally inspected periodically to insure they are functioning properly. For most chemical applications a minimal face velocity of 100 cubic feet per minute (cfm) is required. Modern hoods have flow rate indicators. If the air flow drops below the threshold value, an alarm sounds and an indicator light flashes.

Lab procedures that generate dangerous fumes should always be performed in a hood. Always close the sash as much as possible while still allowing comfortable working conditions.

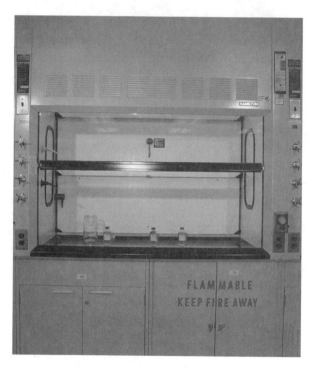

Figure 1-8. Fume hood.

1-4 HANDLING CHEMICALS

All chemicals pose some level of hazard. Even something as common as water can be hazardous under the right conditions (consider someone who can't swim). It is critical that the hazards associated with all chemicals be known before the chemicals are used. The best source of information on chemical hazards is the **material safety data sheet**, commonly referred to as MSDS. A good place to find material safety data sheets is on the internet.

Chemicals, Solutions, and Reagents

In the chemistry lab these terms have specific meanings.

+ **Chemicals** are single chemical compounds of known purity and composition. A chemical label will contain the name and purity. If no purity is given, it can be assumed to be 100%.

+ **Solutions** consist of one chemical (the **solute**) dissolved in another (the **solvent**). A solution label will contain the name of the chemical, its concentration, and the solvent. If no solvent is named, it is assumed to be water.

+ **Reagents** are all prepared chemicals and solutions used to detect, analyze, and make other substances. They can be as simple as a weak acid solution (e.g., 0.10 M HCl) or complex mixtures of a number of chemicals, such as Yamada's Universal Indicator, a solution of five different acid–base indicators.

Chemical Storage in the Lab

Low hazard chemicals, solutions, and reagents are stored on the **reagent bench**. This is also where you will find other supplies that you will need to perform your experiments.

Chemicals, solutions, and reagents that are expensive, rare, or require refrigeration are stored in the preproom. These must be checked out when needed.

More dangerous reagents are normally stored in a hood. This includes concentrated acids, concentrated bases, volatile liquids, and chemical waste.

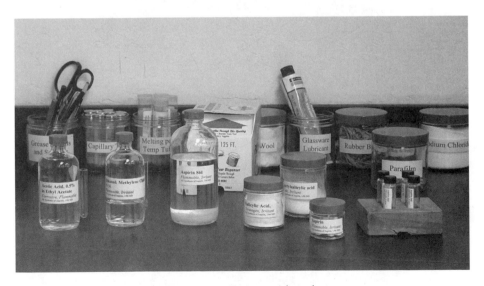

Figure 1-9. A reagent bench.

Obtaining Reagents

Reagent bottles should not be removed from their storage location, especially those stored in a hood. The proper procedure for obtaining a reagent is to take an appropriate container to the reagent bottle and take only what you need. Transporting a large container of any chemical can be hazardous and is to be avoided.

Check the label carefully before you use a reagent. Use of the wrong reagent will ruin your experiment and could result in a serious accident. You also need to make sure you label everything you make and use in the lab. Many accidents result from assumptions made about unlabeled containers.

When using reagent bottles, you must be observant for spills. One common cause of chemical burns in a teaching lab is spilled reagent left on the **outside** of the bottle. It is easy to slop reagent down the outside of the bottle. If you do so, make sure you clean it up. And watch out for wet bottles!

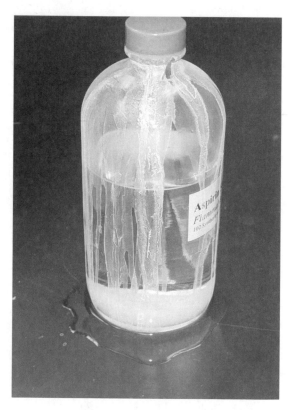

Figure 1-10. A dangerous bottle.

When using reagent bottles, you must also avoid contamination. You must develop habits that will minimize the possibility of contamination.

+   NEVER set the cap to the reagent bottle down. Hold it between the second and third fingers of one hand.

+   NEVER insert objects (including pipets) into reagent bottles. Instead, transfer some of the reagent to a clean beaker and pipet from this container. EXCEPTION: In those cases where there is a designated transfer pipet associated with the reagent bottle, this pipet may be inserted into the bottle.

+   NEVER return unused reagent to the reagent bottle. Dispose of all unused reagent as chemical waste.

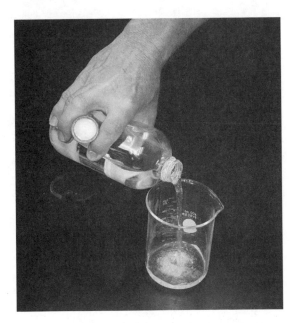

Figure 1-11. Holding a reagent cap while pouring reagent.

Laboratory Safety

1-5 DEALING WITH THE UNEXPECTED

Even in the safest labs, the unexpected will occur. Breaking beakers and chemical spills are not uncommon. Sometimes these events lead to injuries. People get cut or burned. People pass out. Furthermore, no one is at their best when faced with the unexpected. Uncertainty or panic can make the situation worse. The best approach to any unexpected situation is to get help.

Should an accident occur, *immediately notify the instructor.*

Chemical contact can potentially lead to poisoning and/or tissue destruction. Poisoning occurs when chemicals are adsorbed through the skin. *Chemical burns* can be just as nasty as *heat burns* and often cause no pain until after damage is done. Any chemical contact with skin should be treated as a potential chemical burn. The first response to both is the same: *Notify the instructor and run water over the exposed skin for 15 minutes.*

Thermal burns are most commonly the result of contact with hot items such as a hot plate or hot beaker. *Notify the instructor, run water over the exposed skin for 15 minutes and watch for blistering.*

Minor cuts are usually the result of broken glass. Notify the instructor and wash with water until the bleeding stops. Even something as seemingly innocuous as a cut from a broken piece of glass could become very nasty if that glass were contaminated with a dangerous chemical. Let your instructor help judge the severity of any incident.

Major injuries and fainting are uncommon. Should such an event occur, get the instructor immediately.

Alarms sound when there is imminent danger. You will need to evacuate the building immediately. If you are performing an experiment, shut off all utilities (water, power, etc.) and then leave the lab.

Figure 1-12.

1-6 WASTE DISPOSAL

You will need to become familiar with the various kinds of waste generated in a chemistry lab and the proper protocol for disposing of each. These are:

Solid chemical waste. All solid chemicals remaining at the end of the experiment must be put in the designated container. Used transfer pipets are considered to be solid chemical waste and should be disposed of as such.

Liquid organic waste. A separate container is available for liquid organic waste. Never pour organics down the drain.

Acidic and basic water solutions. A separate container is provided for these. Never pour them down the drain.

Heavy metal water solutions. A separate container is provided for heavy metal waste. Never pour these solutions down the drain.

Glass waste. All glass waste must be put in the designated glass waste container. This includes glass with chemicals on it, such as capillary tubes, glass TLC plates, broken flasks, etc.

Garbage. Paper and other normal trash. Never put glass or chemicals in the garbage cans. Never put used glass transfer pipets in the garbage cans.

Drain water. Only neutral water solutions that do not contain heavy metals or organics can be poured down the drain. And never put any solids down the drain!

Figure 1-13. Chemical waste hood.

1-7 CHEMISTRY LAB SAFETY CHECKLIST

Before beginning work in the lab, you should make sure of the following:

+ You have approved safety goggles and use them whenever any experimental work is being performed in the lab.

+ You have a lab coat and use it when required.

+ You are wearing an appropriate pair of shoes.

+ You have gloves and use them when required.

+ You are familiar with the precautions for the chemicals you will be using.

+ You know the location and proper operation of the following.

  a. the hoods

  b. the nearest safety shower

  c. the nearest eyewash station

  d. the first aid box

  e. the exits

  f. the reagent bench

1-8 STUDENT SAFETY AGREEMENT

You must agree to the following seven statements before you will be allowed to do any lab work in our labs. Please read them over and be prepared to indicate your agreement. If you have any concerns regarding these statements, you must discuss them with the course instructor before beginning lab work.

+ I will obtain approved safety goggles and an appropriate lab coat and will wear them at all times when any experimental work is being done by anyone in the lab.

+ I am familiar with the location and proper operation of the safety shower, the eyewash stations, and the first aid box.

+ To the best of my ability, I will obey all instructions concerning the safe performance of experiments. I will use the hood when required, dispose of all chemicals and other materials as instructed, and promptly return all chemicals and reagents to their appropriate place when finished. I will not allow reagents or chemicals to become contaminated.

+ I will protect myself by wearing appropriate clothing in the lab. I realize that I must wear shoes that protect my feet from chemical contact in the event of a spill.

+ I will not attempt any unauthorized experiments nor will I work in the lab without proper supervision.

+ I understand that my behavior in the lab is governed by the University's Code of Conduct and that failure to abide by University and Department safety rules and regulations will be considered a violation of that code and can result in my ejection from the lab.

+ I understand that the University does not provide liability insurance coverage for me and that I am responsible for making arrangements to cover the financial burden of injuries I may incur during this class.

DATA COLLECTION AND ANALYSIS

This chapter discusses a number of techniques for data collection and analysis that you will use frequently in this course. You may already be familiar with this material from previous courses. If so, then this chapter should provide a handy reference during your lab work. If this material is not familiar to you, then you will need to learn it before beginning lab work.

+ Basic mathematical operations.

+ Accuracy and precision.

+ Percent yield.

+ Graphing.

+ Using Excel.

+ Using Vernier's Logger *Pro* software.

2-1 MATH ASSESSMENT EXERCISE

To be successful in a chemistry lab you will need to have certain math skills. This exercise is designed to help you determine if you have those skills. To perform the assessment, time how long it takes for you to answer the following questions. Then check your answers against those given at the end of the chapter.

+ If you can answer all questions correctly in 15 minutes or less, your math skills are sharp and this chapter will be a review.

+ If you struggle to answer some questions and it takes you longer than 30 minutes, you should expect to reference this chapter when writing reports.

+ If you can not answer the questions, you should expect that you will require significant help with the reports and tests.

How many significant figures are in each number?

1. 5.4

2. 4.682×10^7

3. 0.00081

4. 5,280

Perform the following operations.

5. $10^0 = ?$

6. $10^3 \times 10^{-9} = ?$

7. $\log 1000 = ?$

8. How many cups of tequila are in a 1.75 L bottle? (One cup contains 236 mL)

9. Consider the following volume measurements: 24.3 mL, 24.6 mL, 24.4 mL, 24.3 mL, 24.1 mL

   a. Calculate the average volume.

   b. Calculate the standard deviation.

10. Solve the following equation for T.

$$PV = nRT$$

11. The general formula for a linear equation is $y = mx + b$. Draw a graph of this equation and label the graph with each of the terms in the equation (y, m, x, and b).

12. Graph the data in Table 2-1.

Table 2-1. Problem 12 data.

Time (sec)	Absorbance
5	727
10	711
30	630
60	537
100	425
150	325
250	180
350	115
400	91

13. Consider the following reaction.

$$2\,H_2 + O_2 \rightarrow 2\,H_2O$$

If 1.00 gram of elemental hydrogen (H_2) is reacted with excess oxygen and 1.00 gram of water is recovered, what is the percent yield of this reaction?

Define the following terms as they apply in a chemistry lab.

14. Accuracy

15. Precision

16. Error

2-2 BASIC MATHEMATICAL OPERATIONS

Interpreting the results of a chemical experiment frequently requires the use of mathematics. Sometimes this is as simple as dividing two numbers to determine a percent yield. On other occasions, rather complex analyses are required, as with the use of integration to interpret kinetic data. The following is a discussion of the mathematical skills you will need to successfully complete this course.

Making Conversions

Many laboratory problems require conversion of one unit to another: dollars to cents, liters to milliliters, grams to moles. The easy way to make simple conversions is to use a **conversion factor**, a ratio that connects the given unit to the desired unit. The values and units in this ratio are arranged so that, on multiplication, the given unit is eliminated and the desired unit remains.

Conversion factors are obtained from a simple equality. For example, consider the conversion of 20 miles into kilometers (km). We know (or can find in a table) that 1 mile = 1.61 km. This relationship produces two conversion factors.

$$\frac{1\ \text{mile}}{1.61\ \text{km}} = 1 \quad \text{and} \quad \frac{1.61\ \text{km}}{1\ \text{mile}} = 1$$

By multiplying the given unit, 20 miles, by the ratio, 1.61 km/1 mile, we get 32 km:

$$20\ \text{miles} \times \frac{1.61\ \text{km}}{1\ \text{mile}} = 32\ \text{km}$$

Note that 1.61 km is placed on top and 1 mile on the bottom so that the given unit, miles, can cancel, leaving the desired unit, km. If we want to convert 20 km to miles, we put 1 mile on top and 1.61 km on the bottom so that km would cancel, leaving miles:

$$20\ \text{km} \times \frac{1\ \text{mile}}{1.61\ \text{km}} = 12.4\ \text{miles}$$

More complex conversions will involve the use of multiple conversion factors. Any number of them can be strung together to obtain an answer with the desired units. This process is often referred to as "unit analysis" or "the factor–label method."

As an example, consider how many dollar bills laid end to end would be required to circle the earth at the equator. First we need to know that the earth has a circumference at the equator of 24,000 miles and that a dollar bill is 15.5 cm long. The process will require converting miles to feet, feet to inches, inches to cm and finally cm to dollar bills. Equation 2-1 illustrates how this is done.

$$24,000 \text{ miles} \times \frac{5,280 \text{ ft}}{1 \text{ mile}} \times \frac{12 \text{ in}}{1 \text{ ft}} \times \frac{2.54 \text{ cm}}{1 \text{ in}} \times \frac{1 \text{ dollar bill}}{15.5 \text{ cm}} = 249,000,000 \text{ dollar bills} \quad (2\text{-}1)$$

Exponential Numbers and Scientific Notation

The last example demonstrates the problem of writing very large numbers. They take up lots of space and are hard to read. In chemistry we often deal with very large or very small numbers. For example, we say that 602300000000000000000000 atoms comprise a mole of atoms or that green light has a wavelength of .000054 cm. These numbers are rather inconvenient to use as written. To simplify calculations and reduce confusion, we use **scientific notation**. This is a shorthand notation that expresses all those place-holding zeroes as a superscript. The above numbers are written in scientific notation respectively as:

$$6.023 \times 10^{23} \text{ atoms} \quad \text{and} \quad 5.4 \times 10^{-5} \text{ cm}$$

Logarithms

Very large numbers can often be more easily processed by first converting them into logarithms (commonly referred to as logs). Many chemical relationships are mathematically complex and can be better understood if the data is processed using logs. For these reasons the ability to manipulate logs is critical to doing chemistry.

Mathematically, the logarithm of a number is the power to which the base number must be raised in order to produce that number. For example, the logarithm of 1000 (base 10) is 3: $10^3 = 1000$ and $\log_{10}(1000) = 3$.

Base 10 is far and away the most common base used in chemistry. For that reason, it is not necessary to specify base 10. If no base is specified base 10 can be assumed.

The other common base used in chemistry is the natural base, e. In this case, the natural log notation, ln, is used. For example, the natural log of 1000 is 6.907755: $e^{6.907755} = 1000$ and $\ln(1000) = 6.907755$.

Conversion between numbers and their logs are usually achieved using either a calculator or a spreadsheet program such as Excel. The latter is described below. In addition to the inter-conversion, knowledge of two operations is also important.

1. The product of two numbers is the sum of the logs of those numbers.
$$\text{Log}(ab) = \log(a) + \log(b)$$

2. A number raised to a power is that power times the log of that number.
$$\text{Log}(a^3) = 3\log(a)$$

Algebraic Equations

An algebraic equation is a shorthand notation for expressing mathematical equality. For example, a researcher discovers that the mass of any piece of pure iron divided by its volume always gives the same answer, as long as all the pieces of iron are at the same temperature. Such a word description can be shortened to the following:

$$\frac{\text{mass of piece of iron}}{\text{volume of piece of iron}} = \begin{array}{l}\text{a constant number,}\\ \text{regardless of the size}\\ \text{of the iron object}\end{array}$$

This expression can be simplified even further by use of symbols to give:

$$\frac{M}{V} = D$$

where M represents the mass of the iron, V represents its volume and D represents the constant number (known as the **density**). This is a simple algebraic equation. If any two of the above variables are known, the third can always be calculated.

You will use algebraic equations in this course to calculate unknown quantities. Occasionally you will need to rearrange an equation to use it. When attempting to determine the value of a particular symbol in an equation, it is necessary to isolate that symbol on one side of the equation (either side will do).

A general rule to remember is that you can perform a mathematical operation on one side of the equation (add, subtract, multiply, divide, square, etc.) as long as you perform exactly the same operation on the other side.

Example

Every substance has a constant value for density (D in the above equation) at a given temperature. Suppose we know the density of lead to be 11.3 g/mL. We wish to know the mass of a piece of lead but we can only measure its volume with the equipment at hand. Using the equation for density, we can calculate the mass in the following manner:

$$D = \frac{M}{V}$$

We wish to isolate the mass on one side of the equation. This can be done by multiplying both sides by the volume.

$$V \times D = \frac{M}{V} \times V$$

The mass equals the volume times the density. Therefore, multiplying the volume and the density gives the mass of the object.

$$V \times D = M$$

2-3 THE RELIABILITY OF MEASUREMENTS

Experimentation frequently involves making measurements of physical properties. Some measurements will be more reliable than others, but no measurement is absolutely correct. An understanding of the reliability of measurements made in the lab is crucial for the proper interpretation of the results of an experiment. This section will deal with a number of terms and concepts that you will need to understand to properly evaluate the measurements you make.

Experimental Error

In science, the term "error" has a different meaning than in general usage. To most people, an error is a mistake. Thus, "experimental error" is often interpreted as resulting from mistakes made by the experimenter. This is not always the case. The scientific definition of error refers to the uncertainty of results and not necessarily to the cause. Some sources of error are avoidable. Others are not. It is best to avoid thinking of error as "mistakes" but rather as uncertainty or deviations.

THE MEANING OF "ERROR"

A misconception regarding error is that it is **bad**. In fact, error is a property of all measurements. What is important is the **magnitude** of the error associated with a measurement. Whenever a measurement is made in the lab, the degree of error must be determined and then evaluated to see how it affects the interpretation of the results. For every experiment you perform, you must evaluate the errors associated with the measurements and discuss how they may limit the conclusions made.

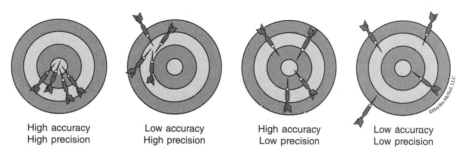

| High accuracy | Low accuracy | High accuracy | Low accuracy |
| High precision | High precision | Low precision | Low precision |

Figure 2-1. Accuracy and precision.

Accuracy and Precision

Accuracy and **precision** are two distinct ideas describing different aspects of a measurement's reliability. **Accuracy** describes how close the measurement comes to the true value. **Precision** describes how close a series of measurements are to each other.

Accuracy and precision are relative terms. We normally talk of the degree of accuracy and the degree of precision. To say that a value is accurate implies a comparison to some standard. The standards are usually based on previous experience with the technique. Unless a verification experiment is being performed, the degree of accuracy of a measurement is determined by reference to the generally accepted accuracy of the technique and a subjective evaluation of the conditions of the measurement.

Since no measurement technique is perfect, repeated measurements of the same quantity usually show some scatter. The size of the scatter is a measure of the precision of the measurements (see Figure 2-1). In reporting the results of a set of measurements we should give the best value for the set. If all the measurements are equally reliable, then the best value is the arithmetic mean, more commonly known as the average value. The average is the sum of all the values divided by the number of values. The mathematical expression for this operation is

$$\text{average} = \bar{x} = \frac{\sum_i X_i}{n} \qquad (2\text{-}2)$$

For example, suppose you weighed the same crucible four times and obtained the values presented in Table 2-2. The best value for the mass of the crucible is 21.18 g, the average of the four weighings.

Table 2-2. Crucible weighings.

Trial	Value
1st Weighing	21.24 g
2nd Weighing	21.11 g
3rd Weighing	21.22 g
4th Weighing	21.16 g
Average Value	**21.18 g**

Clearly, this average value still has some uncertainty in it. After all, at no time was the mass of the crucible actually measured to be 21.18 g. Precision is a measure of the scatter in a set of data. The less the scatter, the more precise the data are.

Unlike accuracy, the precision of a data set can readily be measured. First, the deviation of each value from the average is determined.

$$\text{deviation} = |x_i - \bar{x}| \qquad (2\text{-}3)$$

Note the absolute value bars. Deviations are always positive, regardless of the direction of the deviation. Table 2-3 shows the calculation of the deviations for the data in Table 2-2.

Table 2-3. Calculating deviations.

Trial	$X_i - \bar{X}$	Deviation
1st Weighing	|21.24 – 21.18|	= 0.06
2nd Weighing	|21.11 – 21.18|	= 0.07
3rd Weighing	|21.22 – 21.18|	= 0.04
4th Weighing	|21.16 – 21.18|	= 0.02

The deviations are inspected to determine if any of the measurements are questionable. A questionable measurement is one with a deviation significantly larger than the other deviations. Questionable measurements may need to be discarded. This would be determined by inspecting the lab notebook to see if any unusual events occurred that could explain the deviation.

The deviations are then combined to produce a measure of the precision of the data set.

The most common method of expressing the precision of a series of repetitive measurements is the **standard deviation**. This operation produces a number that is a measure of how closely all values are clustered around the average value. In general, the standard deviation is a good predictor of the probable range of values that would be obtained from additional measurements.

$$\text{standard deviation} = s = \sqrt{\frac{\sum_i (x_i - \overline{x})^2}{n-1}} \qquad (2\text{-}4)$$

To see how the calculation of a standard deviation works, consider the data presented in Table 2-2. The deviations can be used as calculated in Table 2-3.

$$s = \sqrt{\frac{\sum_i (x_i - \overline{x})^2}{n-1}} = \sqrt{\frac{(0.06^2 + 0.07^2 + 0.04^2 + 0.02^2)}{4-1}} = 0.06 \qquad (2\text{-}5)$$

The precision of a quantity that was measured repetitively is usually expressed by presenting both the average value and the standard deviation. For our example, this would be reported as

$$21.18 \pm 0.06 \text{ g}$$

This representation gives us not only the best value for the measurements, but some indication of the uncertainty of the best value. In this case, the number 21.18 g for the mass of the crucible is uncertain to ± 0.06 g.

Another method of expressing the precision of measurements is the **relative standard deviation**. This is computed by comparing the standard deviation to the average value.

$$\text{relative standard deviation} = \frac{s}{\overline{x}} \qquad (2\text{-}6)$$

Relative standard deviation is most useful for comparing the precision of measured numbers that differ significantly in magnitude. For example, which set of measurements is more precise, a series of absorbencies that produces a value of 1.20 ± 0.09 or another set with a value of 0.341 ± 0.05? Is it the second set with the smaller standard deviation? Let's look at the relative standard deviations.

$$\text{for } 1.20 \pm 0.09, \quad \frac{0.09}{1.2} = 0.08$$

$$\text{and}$$

$$\text{for } 0.341 \pm 0.05, \quad \frac{0.05}{0.341} = 0.15$$

The first set of measurements is more precise.

Finally, relative standard deviations are sometimes presented as **percent relative standard deviations.** This is obtained by taking the relative standard deviation and multiplying by 100%. Thus, the above relative standard deviations become 8% and 15%, respectively.

Significant Figures

Anytime a measurement is made, there is a limit to the number of digits that can be read. This determines the number of significant figures for measurements made with that device. For example, a car odometer measures to the nearest 0.1 mile. With this device, a distance of 50 miles could be measured to three significant figures. When used properly, a 10 mL volumetric pipet measures ten-milliliter samples to exactly 10.00 mL, four significant figures.

The number of significant figures in a measurement will, in turn, limit the number of significant figures for any other numbers calculated using that number. As an example of significant figures, consider how reliably you can state your weight. If you say, "I weigh 160 lb," does this mean exactly 160 lb or does it mean 160 ± 1–2 lb? If you know your weight so reliably that you can say it is 160.000 lb, we say you know it to six significant figures. If you know your weight reliably enough to say you weigh 160 lb ± a few ounces or so, we say you know it to three significant figures. **In making calculations with measured quantities such as your weight, you cannot report your answer to more significant figures than is merited by the least reliable of the measured quantities used.** For example, if you know your weight reliably to be 160 lb and the volume of your body reliably to be 75 liters, you can calculate the density of your body by dividing your weight by your volume:

$$\frac{160 \text{ lb}}{75 \text{ L}} = 2.1 \frac{\text{lb}}{\text{L}}$$

You cannot correctly report your density to more than two significant figures since the least reliable of the quantities involved in the calculation has only two significant figures. Thus you might correctly say that your density is 2.1 lb/L but you would be incorrect to say, on the basis of these numbers and calculations, that your density is 2.13 or 2.1333 lb/L.

2-4 DETERMINING PERCENT YIELD

In theory, all chemical reactions should give a 100% yield. In practice, this is not true. There are many reasons why the yield of a reaction will be different than 100%. The yield will be less than 100% if material is lost during the reaction or during the recovery process. It is also possible that the reaction itself did not go to completion. Yields that appear to be greater than 100% are also possible if the product is not pure.

In theory, a **percent yield** calculation is rather simple. You are comparing the amount of product obtained, the experimental yield, to the amount of product you predict you would obtain if the reaction were 100% complete and there were no losses.

$$\% \text{ yield} = \frac{\text{experimental yield}}{\text{theoretical yield}} \times 100\% \qquad (2\text{-}7)$$

In practice, there are tricks to determining a percent yield. First, a percent yield is a ratio and cannot have units. This means that the experimental yield and theoretical yield values must use the same units. Most commonly moles are used, but if the formulas of the compounds do not change, the calculation will work with grams.

To determine the experimental yield, the mass of product is determined. If the molar mass is known, then this mass is converted into moles.

$$\text{mass}_{\text{product}} \times \frac{1}{\text{MM}_{\text{product}}} = \text{exp. moles}_{\text{product}} \qquad (2\text{-}8)$$

The theoretical yield is determined from the moles of product predicted based on the chemical equation. For this determination one must use the coefficients in the chemical reaction.

$$\text{moles}_{\text{reactant}} \text{ used} \times \frac{\text{moles}_{\text{product}} \text{ from equation}}{\text{moles}_{\text{reactant}} \text{ from equation}} = \text{theoretical moles}_{\text{product}} \qquad (2\text{-}9)$$

As an example of a percent yield calculation consider making water and carbon dioxide from glucose and oxygen.

$$C_6H_{12}O_6 + 6\,O_2 \rightarrow 6\,CO_2 + 6\,H_2O$$

Say you start with 9.00 grams of glucose and end up with 4.32 grams of water.
What is your percent yield?
That 9.00 grams of glucose is 0.0500 moles.

$$9.00 \text{ grams of glucose used} \times \frac{1 \text{ mole of glucose}}{180 \text{ grams of glucose}} = 0.0500 \text{ moles of glucose used}$$

The experimental yield is 0.240 moles of water.

$$4.32 \text{ grams H}_2\text{O} \times \frac{1 \text{ mole H}_2\text{O}}{18.02 \text{ grams of glucose}} = 0.240 \text{ moles H}_2\text{O}$$

Your theoretical yield is 0.300 moles of water.

$$0.0500 \text{ moles glucose used} \times \frac{6 \text{ moles water}}{1 \text{ mole glucose}} = 0.300 \text{ moles of water produced (theor.)}$$

Finally,

$$\% \text{ yield} = \frac{0.240 \text{ moles of water obtained}}{0.300 \text{ moles of water theorectically made}} \times 100\% = 80.0\% \text{ yield}$$

Figure 2-2. Sample percent yield calculation.

2·5 GRAPHING

The relationship between various experimental parameters is often best understood by graphing the data obtained. Sometimes a graph is needed to obtain the desired experimental result. The value of graphical analysis is strongly dependent on the quality of data used and the degree of care employed in constructing the graph. Graphs should be constructed in such a manner that they do not reduce the accuracy and precision of the data presented. The following graphing pointers are presented with this goal in mind.

1. Select Your Platform

Graphs can be made either by hand or using computer programs. Graphs constructed while in the lab will often be made by hand. It's always a good idea to graph data as the experiment progresses. This allows for the identification of problems as they occur. It is also sometimes necessary to graph data to determine what to do next. Final graphs intended for inclusion in reports or posters can be made by hand, but are usually better if generated using a computer.

Table 2-4. Dye bleaching data.

Time (sec)	Absorbance
10	0.907
30	0.844
60	0.753
90	0.678
120	0.602
150	0.544
180	0.485
210	0.433
240	0.383
270	0.344
300	0.315
330	0.283
360	0.248
390	0.226

Using a computer will void the need to use graph paper, but may generate other problems. If you are unfamiliar with the operation of the program you could end up generating an inaccurate or misleading graph. Conversely, computer generated graphs allow for more complex manipulation of data. Graphical presentations can be further analyzed to produce more convincing arguments. The choice of hand-drawn or computer-generated graphs will depend on the requirements of the particular experiment and the course.

2. Handmade Graphs

If you construct your graph by hand, you will need graph paper to ensure that your data points are as accurately placed as possible. The following discusses how to construct a suitable graph.

Select the axes. A two-dimensional graph will have two scales. The x-axis, or abscissa, runs left to right across the graph. The y-axis, or ordinate, runs up and down. Normally, the *independent variable* is plotted along the x-axis and the *dependent variable* on the y-axis. The independent variable is the one for which you set the value when you perform the experiment. The dependent variable is the data obtained as a result of your selection of the independent variable. Consider the data presented in Table 2-4. This data was collected by placing the sample in a spectrophotometer and then reading the absorbance at specific times. The time is the independent variable. The values were selected by the experimenter and will be placed along the bottom of the graph. The absorbance is the dependent variable. It was read from the machine at the chosen times. The absorbance will be plotted up and down.

Determine scale ranges. To ensure maximum usefulness of your graph, you need to select scales that will allow your graph to be as big as possible. Begin by identifying, for each range, the largest and smallest values in the data set. In Table 2-4, these are 10 and 390 for the times and 0.907 and 0.226 for the absorbance. Next, identify how many small divisions are available for each axis on the graph paper available to you. Finally, determine the nearest integral number of units per graph division. Once the values for each division have been determined, draw the axes on the graph and label some major lines with their values. See Figure 2-3 for an example.

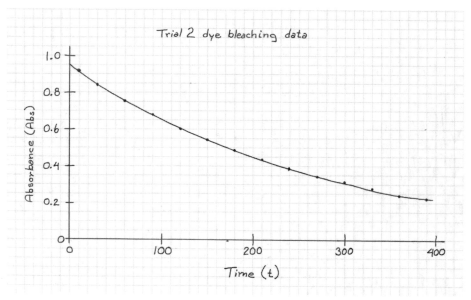

Figure 2-3. A hand-drawn graph.

Plot the data. Place a small dot, or x, at the location of each of the data points. After all the data have been plotted, draw the smoothest curve possible through all your points. Do not simply connect the points.

Label the graph. The graph will not be complete until you have titled it and labeled each of the axes. Don't forget to include the units. Again, see Figure 2-3 for an example.

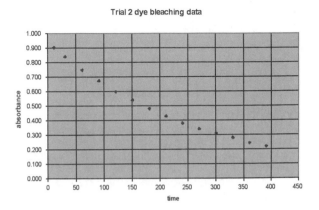

Figure 2-4. A computer-generated graph.

3. Computer-Made Graphs

These are ideal for the formal presentation of data if they present the data in the proper context and with sufficient detail. The first consideration is the suitability of the software. There are many graphing programs available with many different capabilities. A suitable program will allow the user to perform the same manipulations described for hand graphing. It will also allow for the interpolation of values, if required, with the same accuracy as the data used. The most common spreadsheet program is Microsoft's Excel, which is discussed in the next section.

2-6 DATA MANAGEMENT USING EXCEL

Excel is the spreadsheet component of Microsoft Office and is quite common. It is designed primarily for use with financial data but can be made to work for scientific applications. It is most useful for performing repetitive calculations on large data sets, for graphing experimental data and for generating professional looking results tables. The following is a brief and rather cursory introduction to some of the more useful features of Excel. All references are to the version of Excel contained in Office 2010.

1. Basic Data Entry

The spreadsheet consists of data cells arranged in columns and rows. Columns are identified by letters and rows by numbers. Thus, the first cell in the upper left hand corner is cell A1. There are two ways to enter data into a cell. Select the cell then double click on it to get a cursor in the cell. Alternately, select the cell and type in the edit bar at the top of the spreadsheet.

Excel treats cell contents as either numbers or labels. If you enter a number Excel will treat it as a number. If you enter any character other than a number Excel will treat it as a label. Mixed numbers and letters are labels. If you wish to enter a number but have it treated as a label, start the entry with an apostrophe.

2. Basic Data Manipulation

You can have Excel perform mathematical operations by using equations. For example, consider a situation where you need to know the density of a liquid. Density is mass per unit volume.

$$Density = \frac{mass}{volume}$$

To create this equation in Exel, start by entering the values for mass and volume into appropriately labeled cells. Next, in the cell where you want the density displayed, put the equation. Start with an equal sign (see Figure 2-5). Excel recognizes standard operators: addition (+), subtraction (–), multiplication (*), division (/), and power (^). You can also nest calculations using parentheses. Notice that the equation appears in the edit bar.

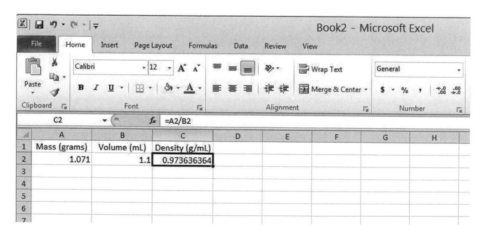

Figure 2-5. Simple calculation in Excel.

3. Copying Formulas

When you copy a cell containing an equation you will copy the equation. Excel will automatically change the cell references to correspond to the new cell you're copying into (Figure 2-6). When you copy a formula, you may paste it into multiple cells by selecting all the cells you want the formula to appear in.

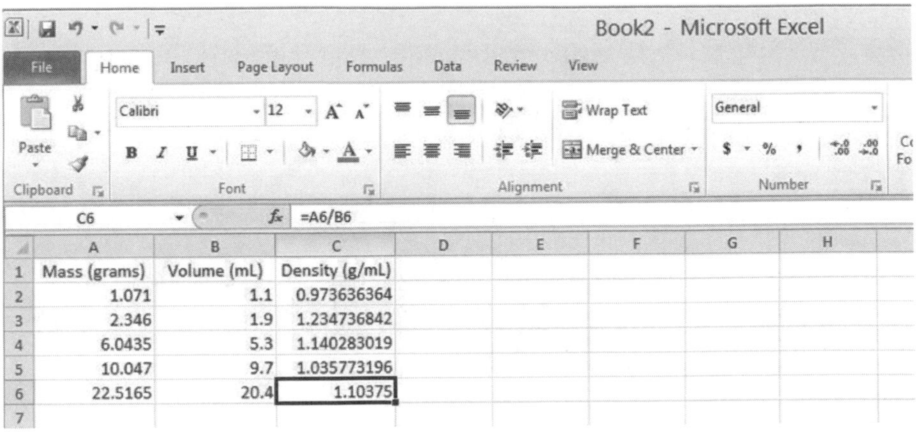

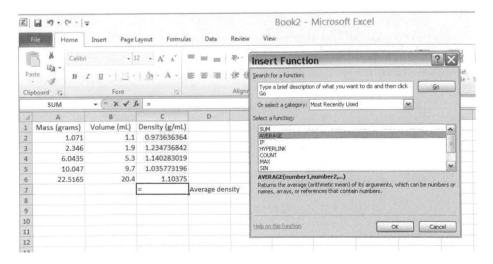

Figure 2-6. Copying formulas.

4. Using Functions

Excel contains many functions for your use. To access the function menu, double click on the *fx* symbol on the edit bar. A function consists of a function name followed by parameters in parentheses. The parameters are usually the cells to be included in the function calculation. For example, the equation for calculating the average area as shown in Figure 2-7 will be =AVERAGE(C2:C6). Note that the colon indicates an inclusive range of cells (C2 through C6).

Figure 2-7. Functions in Excel.

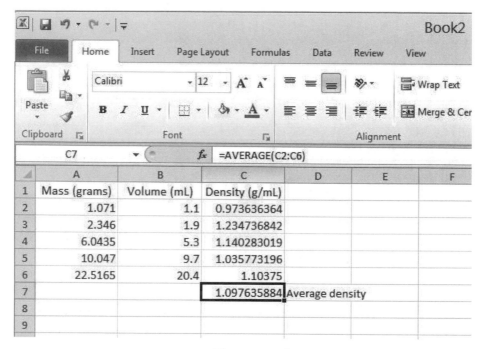

Figure 2-8. The average function.

5. Common Excel Functions

The following Excel functions will be useful in this course.

AVERAGE(cell1:cell2)—used to average a set of numbers. All numbers from the designated cell1 through the designated cell2 inclusive will be averaged. This was discussed in the previous section.

SUM(cell1:cell2)—used to add up a set of numbers. Follows the same general format as the average formula.

The following functions can be used for a specific number. They can also be used to perform the operation on the number in a particular cell by replacing "number" in the formula with the cell address.

LN(number)—calculates the natural log of the number.

EXP(number)—calculates e raised to the power of the number.

LOG10(number)—calculates the base 10 log of the number.

10^(number)—calculates 10 raised to the power of the number.

6. Toolbars

Figure 2-9 highlights some possibly useful features of the Excel toolbar. Highlight the cells you want to format and then select the desired formatting function.

Change font and font size—for changing the style and size of the cell contents.

Change number and label type—for changing numbers into labels and changing the way numbers are displayed (e.g., as percent).

Change decimal places displayed—for setting the number of decimal places displayed in the cell.

Change text placement in cell—for changing the justification of the cell contents (left, right, top, bottom).

Change font color—for changing the color of the cell contents.

Change cell fill color—for changing the background color of the cell.

Borders—for drawing lines around sets of data. Select the arrow to the right of the box to get more options. Select "more borders" from the bottom of the drop down menu to access all the options available. Borders will be drawn around the collection of highlighted cells.

One commonly used effect is to put labels in cells that have white text on a black background. You can do this by setting the fill color to black and the text color to white.

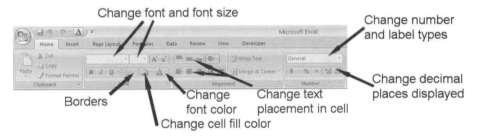

Figure 2-9. Excel toolbars.

7. Graphing Data

Excel can graph columns of data. It will graph one column against one or more other columns. The organization of the data is critical to the appearance of the graph you produce. The following is a description of how to generate a linear graph using the Office 2010 version of Excel.

 Setting up the graph. Highlight the range of cells you want to graph. Include the labels if you want the graph labeled. Under the "insert" tab select the scatter type plot as shown in Figure 2-10.

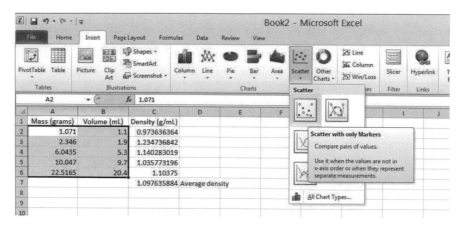

Figure 2-10. Selecting the "scatter" type of graph.

Once you have created the graph you can edit it. To access the chart tools, select the graph and then the "layout" tab. Figure 2-11 shows the chart title tab.

Adding a trend line. For linear relationships a trend line can be quite useful. It provides the slope and a measure of how close the points actually fit the line. To add a trend line, right click on one of the data points. Figure 2-12 shows the menu that will appear. Select "Add Trendline." On the next menu (Figure 2-13), you will need to select the two boxes at the bottom to get an equation and an R2 value to be displayed. Figure 2-14 shows the result.

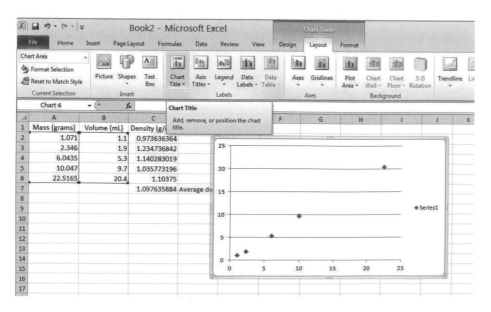

Figure 2-11.

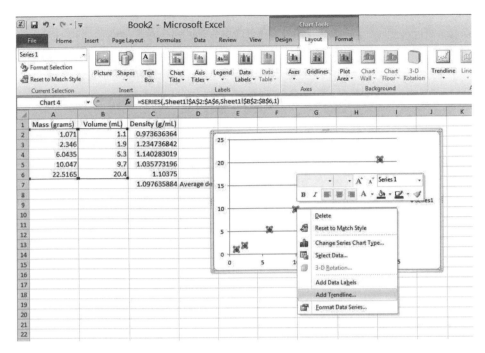

Figure 2-12.

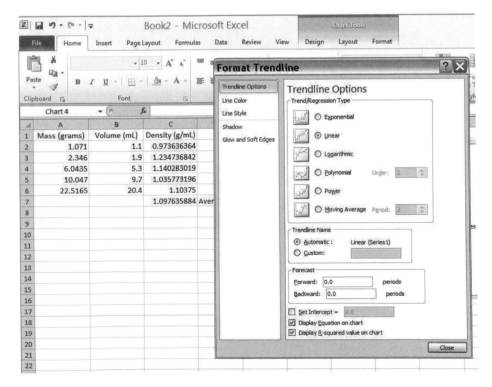

Figure 2-13.

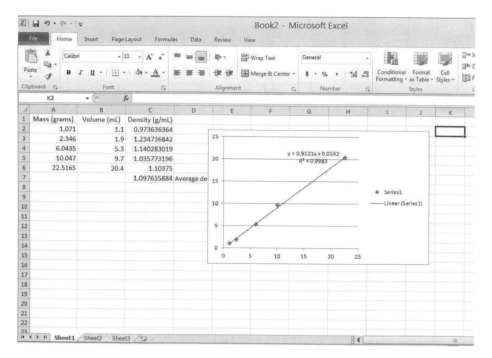

Figure 2-14.

8. Practice Problem

A good way to practice setting up an Excel spreadsheet is to create a molar mass calculator. This will come in handy over the course of the semester. Figure 2-15 shows what such a file might look like. It demonstrates the calculation for sulfuric acid, H_2SO_4. Column B contains atomic masses copied from a periodic chart or atomic mass table. In column C the user enters the number of atoms in the molecule. Column D contains a formula multiplying the number in column B by the number in column C (e.g., =B4*C4). The formula in cell D2 sums all the numbers in column D. Try creating your own molar mass calculator.

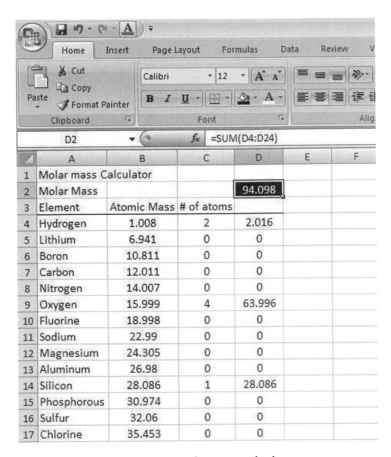

Figure 2-15. A molar mass calculator.

2-7 DATA ACQUISITION USING LOGGER *PRO*

Until the advent of computers all instruments used in chemical laboratories were stand-alone devices. Measurements were read from the instrument, recorded by hand in a data notebook, and then processed by hand, often with the aid of a slide rule or calculator. Recent developments in computer technology now make it possible to import measurements directly into data management programs. In chemistry, the future of instrumentation is intimately tied to the use of computers and data management programs.

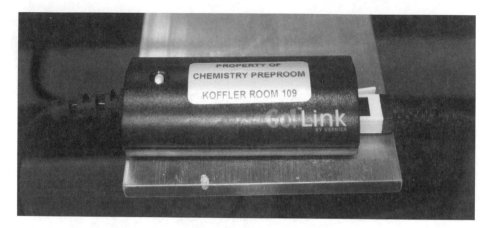

Figure 2-16. Go!Link.

You will have available for your use hardware and software marketed by the Vernier Corporation. The software is known as **Logger *Pro***. The hardware is a collection of instruments that interface with a computer. Some of the instruments (thermometers and spectrometers) will plug directly into a USB port on a computer. Others (pH electrodes, ISEs, pressure sensors) will plug into a device Vernier calls the **Go!Link** which itself plugs into the USB port (Figure 2-16). In all cases the data generated by the instrument will be imported into the Logger *Pro* software where you will then be able to manipulate them to meet your needs. In some cases you will be able to prepare your data tables and graphs directly in Logger *Pro*. In other cases you may need to export the data to Excel for further manipulation.

The Logger *Pro* software is available to be loaded onto personal computers. Should you choose to do so you will then be able to connect the probes directly to your own laptop and save the data there. This will also enable you to use the Logger *Pro* data manipulation features when you are no longer in the lab. If you are interested in this option, consult your instructor.

Logger *Pro*

Initializing Logger Pro *(getting it running)*

1. Make sure the computer is running.

2. Make sure the required instruments are connected to a USB port.

3. Start the software by selecting the Logger *Pro* Icon: Logger Pro 3.8.3

When you load up Logger *Pro* you will get a screen that looks something like Figure 2-17. The box on the bottom left identifies the probe. The spreadsheet on the left is where data will be entered. The graph on the right is where the data will be plotted.

Initially the program will be in standby mode. It will not begin recording data until you select the ▶Collect button from the toolbar (the green button).

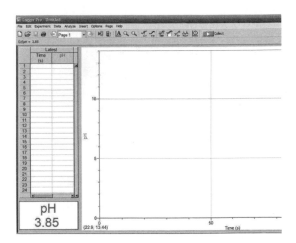

Figure 2-17. Initial Logger *Pro* screen.

Recording Data Over Time

The Logger *Pro* default data collection mode is to record the input from the probe at set time intervals. The default interval is 2 seconds. Figure 2-18 shows what this looks like. Data collection and recording begins when the ▶Collect button is pushed. In the example shown here every two seconds the temperature was entered into the spreadsheet and also plotted on the graph. Data collection and recording will continue until the ■Stop button is pushed.

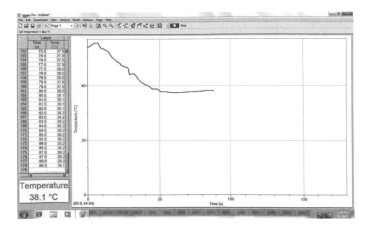

Figure 2-18. Recording data over time.

To change the default time interval select Experiment then Data Collection (Figure 2-19). You will be presented with the option to change the units of time and the frequency of sampling.

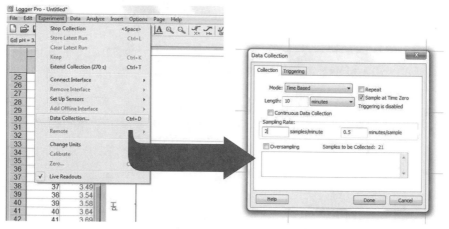

Figure 2-19. Changing data collection frequency.

Recording Data as Events

Logger *Pro* can also be configured to record measurements only when prompted. When in this mode, data is not recorded until you say so. This change is also configured through the Data collection dialog box. Figure 2-20 shows this control.

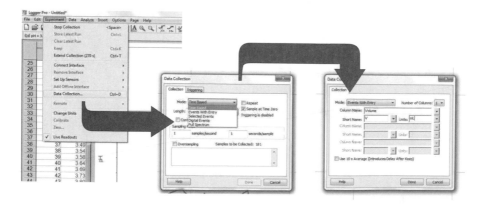

Figure 2-20. Changing to data collection by event.

Figure 2-21 shows Logger *Pro* configured to collect data by event. Notice in the figure that the ▶Collect button has already been selected and the instrument is actively measuring pH. To record data it is necessary to select the ⊛Keep button from the tool bar. When you do so, you will receive a prompt to enter the independent variable value (in this case, volume).

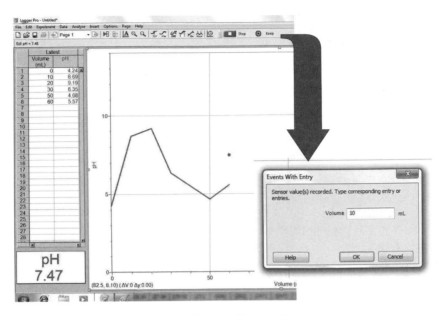

Figure 2-21. Data collection by event.

Saving Data

Logger *Pro* saves data in files having a .cmbl extension. These files can only be opened and used in Logger *Pro*. If you have Logger *Pro* loaded on your computer you can open the .cmbl files and work with them. Figure 2-22 shows the "Save As" dialog box.

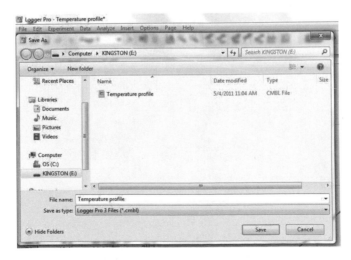

Figure 2-22. Saving a Logger *Pro* data file.

Data Collection and Analysis

In the absence of the Logger *Pro* software, the best way to handle data is to copy and paste it into a spreadsheet program like Excel. Use the cursor to highlight the data in the spreadsheet. Copy and paste into a blank spreadsheet in Excel. If you single click on the column heading you will select the entire column. This makes data transfer much easier when you have hundreds of lines of data. If you hold down the shift key you can select multiple columns to copy.

WARNING

You cannot save files to the lab computers. This is to prevent the accidental infection with a virus. If you are using Logger *Pro* on a lab computer, you will need to save the file to a jump drive that you will need to provide. Of course, if you are running Logger *Pro* on your laptop you won't face this limitation.

Data Collection Probes

There are a number of sensors that can be used with Logger *Pro* to collect and process data. Some plug directly into a USB port on a computer. Others are routed through a GO!Link Some also require an electrode amplifier. A summary is given here. Details on the use of the sensors and the manipulation of Logger *Pro* are given where indicated.

Table 2-5. Logger *Pro* Sensors

Sensor	Connection	Use
Thermometer	USB direct.	Used like a normal thermometer. Logger *Pro* recognizes the thermometer and displays the temperature.
High temperature thermometer	Requires a GO!Link.	Used like a normal thermometer. Logger *Pro* recognizes the thermometer and displays the temperature.
Spectrometer	USB direct	Described in Chapter 8.
Conductivity probe	Requires a GO!Link.	Described in Chapter 10.
pH electrode	Requires an electrode amplifier and a GO!Link.	Described in Chapter 9.
Ion-selective electrode	Requires an electrode amplifier and a GO!Link.	Described in Chapter 9.
Gas pressure sensor	Requires a GO!Link.	Logger *Pro* recognizes the probe and displays the pressure in kilopascals.

2-8 MATH ASSESSMENT EXERCISE ANSWERS

1. 2

2. 4

3. 2. None of the zeros is significant.

4. 3 or 4. The lack of a decimal point makes the significance of the 0 undetermined.

5. 1. Any number raised to the 0 power is 1.

6. 10^{-6}. To multiply exponential numbers, add the exponents.

7. 3

8. $1.75\ \text{L} \times \dfrac{1{,}000\ \text{mL}}{\text{L}} \times \dfrac{1\ \text{cup}}{236\ \text{mL}} = 7.42\ \text{cups}$

9. average = 24.3

    Standard deviation = calculated answer of 0.18 which is more correctly reported as 0.2

10. $T = \dfrac{PV}{nR}$

11.

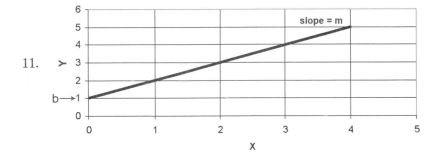

linear equation

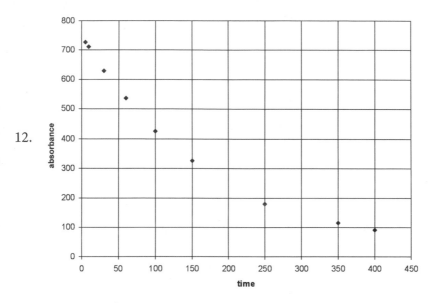

Problem 12 graph

12.

13.

$$1.00 \text{ g H}_2 \times \frac{1 \text{ mol H}_2}{2.016 \text{ g H}_2} \times \frac{1 \text{ mol H}_2\text{O}}{1 \text{ mol H}_2} \times \frac{18.014 \text{ g H}_2\text{O}}{1 \text{ mol H}_2\text{O}}$$

$$= 8.94 \text{ g H}_2\text{O theoretical yield}$$

$$\frac{1.00 \text{ g H}_2\text{O experimental yield}}{8.94 \text{ g H}_2\text{O theoretical yield}} = 11.2\% \text{ yield}$$

14. Accuracy: a measure of how close a value is to the actual value.

15. Precision: a measure of how close a series of values are to each other.

16. Error: a measure of the uncertainty associated with a value.

COMMUNICATING EXPERIMENTAL RESULTS

Scientific experimentation is worthless if the results are not credible and can not be shared with others. Learning how to properly record and present the results of experiments is a critical component of learning how to work in a lab. This chapter presents the following aspects of communicating experimental results.

* Proper use of a laboratory notebook.

* Proper reporting of experimental outcomes.

* The Science Writing Heuristic.

* Literature-style report writing.

A scientific paper is a formal argument. Like any argument, it is of little or no value if it is not convincing. The ability to read and write analytical arguments is critical to most professional endeavors. An important part of learning to work in a chemistry lab is to develop these skills. The material presented here is designed to help you learn how to effectively make a scientific argument, how to properly keep a laboratory notebook, and how to report your findings in a scientific paper. Regarding the last objective, two different kinds of reporting are described. One is the Science Writing Heuristic, a writing method designed to help the student develop the critical thinking skills required in a science laboratory. The other is based on the writing method employed by scientific journals.

SCIENTIFIC INTEGRITY IS FRAGILE

There must never be any doubt that the observer is reporting what was actually observed. Thus, attention to form and detail is critical.

3-1 MAKING AND RECORDING OBSERVATIONS

When conducting an experiment, a chemist performs one or more operations and observes what happens. She or he looks for changes in the system. By observing the changes that occur (or do not occur) the chemist is able to draw conclusions about the nature of the materials involved. Thus **"observation"** is a key concept in the laboratory. Of course, to determine that a change has occurred, one must have detailed knowledge of the initial conditions. The observing must begin before any operations are performed.

The observations made during the course of an experiment can be broadly categorized as either "description" or "measurement." **Descriptions** are the somewhat subjective observations made with the five senses and include such things as color, odor, clarity, and texture. **Measurements** are objective observations that require taking numerical readings from a measuring device.

Making observations is only a part of the process. Equally important is recording them for later reference. Depending on memory is a potentially disastrous mistake too often made by many scientists as well as students. All observations *must* be recorded at the time they are made and to the degree of detail with which they are made. Learning to faithfully and reliably record observations is an important part of learning to work in a lab. Standard practice in all fields of science and engineering is the use of a **lab notebook**.

Descriptions

Descriptive observations are not easy to make. The quality of conclusions drawn from observations depends on how detailed the observations are. For example, if you were to witness a hit-and-run accident, the police would want a description of the vehicle. The response "it was a white car" would not be very useful because there are hundreds of white cars out there. The police would want more details such as the make, model, year, distinguishing marks and/or unusual characteristics (e.g., a broken tail light) and a description of the driver. Likewise, in the lab, you will be expected to observe as much detail as you can. To say that the solution in a test tube is "blue" will not be sufficient. What shade of blue is it? How dark is it? Is it transparent? See any solid? Does it have an odor? Is it hot or cold?

Separating observations from conclusions is important. We have spent our entire lives making decisions based on our observations. As very young children, many of us learned the association between fire and heat by experimentation. It is common for a one-year-old to try to "touch" the flame on a birthday candle. Two-year-olds rarely try this.

You are beginning this course with a large collection of such observations which are often referred to as "common sense." Your mind continuously draws conclusions based on these observations, often without your conscious realization. For example, if you drop a glass object and hear a crash, you assume the glass has broken. You don't need to look for the evidence of the broken glass as your stored observations of the sound made by breaking glass allows you to conclude the object is broken.

When making **observations** in the lab, you need to be aware of assumptions you make based on previous observations. Sometimes they can lead you in the wrong direction. It is **possible** that the glass object did not break and the sound was made by something else. Do not confuse **observations** with **conclusions**. Save your conclusions and assumptions for your discussion.

Measurements

Measurement observations are also not easy. There is more to it than simply recording the numbers. No matter how accurate the instrument, there is a limit to the reliability of any measurement made. All reported measurements should indicate the limit of accuracy as well as the value of the measured quantity. Thus, you need to develop the habit of paying close attention to **significant figures**.

In addition to significant figures, one must also be aware of the **units of measurement**. Any reported value is meaningless unless it is labeled with the correct units. If the weatherman says the temperature in Kansas is 35 degrees, you would not know if Kansans were freezing or sweating unless he specified degrees Fahrenheit or degrees centigrade ($35°C = 95°F$). If you were preparing a meal and the recipe called for "one salt" you would probably be upset. You would not know if the author meant 1 teaspoon, 1 tablespoon, or even 1 cup! Likewise you cannot assume that anyone who reads your reported values will automatically know what units you used.

When reporting experimental data, ALL results MUST contain the correct units and the correct number of significant figures.

3-2 THE LABORATORY NOTEBOOK

Why Keep a Notebook?

The **laboratory notebook** is one of the scientist's most valuable tools. It provides a convenient and easy-to-find place to record everything that happens in the lab. As such, it is a permanent record of the scientist's mental and physical activities. The process of recording observations in the notebook helps to ensure that all necessary observations are made. It also helps the scientist begin the process of organizing and summarizing the data needed to reach a conclusion.

In an industrial environment, scientists are usually given strict guidelines for maintaining laboratory notebooks. A scientist's ability to keep a notebook can directly affect employment and advancement opportunities. It is not unusual for lawyers to subpoena laboratory notebooks to help resolve lawsuits involving liability issues and patent rights. In the academic world the notebook is also critical. When performing original research, the notebook will be the prime source of information required to write a thesis, dissertation, or technical paper.

Your lab notebook will be your primary source of information for the reports you write. The time you spend on your reports will be inversely related to the quality of the notebook you keep. If it is well organized and if you give it sufficient attention in the lab, you will find that your reports will flow directly from it.

Figure 3-1. A laboratory notebook.

What Kind of Notebook?

You need to make sure the notebook you choose is appropriate for its intended use. There are certain characteristics that will make it more valuable to you. The following are highly recommended:

- 5 pages per week of experimental work.

- Carbonless duplicate pages. This will allow you to append copies of your notebook entries to lab reports, should they be required. The originals should *never* be removed from the notebook.

- Square-grid ruling. This is preferable to regular notebook line ruling as it makes it easier to draw figures and preliminary graphs as you work in the lab.

- Water repellent cover to resist the inevitable minor laboratory spills.

- Unique appearance. It should be clearly identifiable to reduce the risk of losing or misplacing it.

Using Your Notebook

The first issue to address is what to write with. Your choices are pencil and ink. There are three major reasons to avoid using pencil in a lab notebook. First, pencil does not photocopy well. Even if you are using a notebook that automatically duplicates entries, you may need to make more copies. For example, you may need to exchange observations with your lab partners. Photocopies that can not be read are a time-consuming annoyance. Second, pencil is easily smudged. This also aggravates the problem of using the notebook entries. But the most important reason is integrity. Because pencil can be erased, and the data rewritten, the authenticity of the data can be questioned. Once lost, a scientist's credibility is very difficult to recover.

All entries in your notebook must be in non-erasable ink. Water soluble ink is a bad idea because spills and splashes are common in a chemistry lab. A blue or black ballpoint pen is recommended.

Figure 3-2. A laboratory notebook in use.

Begin your notebook by creating a title page and table of contents. This should include your name, the course and section number, your instructor's name, the lab room, and the term. The experiments should be entered into the table of contents as you perform them. The title page and table of contents can both be on the same page, as long as you leave room to enter titles for all experiments to be performed.

Each week, start a new page with the name of the experiment, the date and time, and the name of any partners you may be working with. Any anomalies from the title page must also be entered (e.g., if a substitute instructor is present or if you are making up the experiment in a lab other than your own). Don't forget to make an entry in the table of contents as well.

You will then describe everything you observe. Measurements must be recorded and properly labeled. Repeated measurements should be organized into tables. Observations should be recorded in as much detail as practical. Pictures sometimes make a better record than written descriptions. Remember that to be able to describe any changes that occur, you will need to have accurate descriptions of the starting conditions as well as the ending conditions.

When you have completed all experimental work, sign and date your lab notebook. Then show it to your instructor to confirm that you have the data you need. Finally, to guarantee the authenticity of your work, have the lab instructor initial your notebook.

Summary of Notebook Use

+ Enter the experiment title into the table of contents.

+ Start at the top of a new page with the experiment title. Continue with the date, time, names of partners (if any), and any special circumstances (e.g., a make-up lab).

+ Record all observations, measurements, and descriptions of procedures or techniques that deviate from those presented in the instructions.

+ When done working for the day, sign and date below the last entry.

+ Have the lab instructor initial next to your signature.

3-3 WRITING LAB REPORTS: GENERAL COMMENTS

There are three primary reasons for requiring you to write reports. First and foremost is to learn how scientific experiments are commonly reported. Your reports will follow current practice in science and engineering. The format presented here is generally common to all scientific fields. By writing these reports you will be better prepared to both read and write technical reports in your own major.

Next is to require you to analytically reflect on your laboratory experiences with the goal of improving your understanding of the experiment. A report is a highly formatted procedure for processing the results of laboratory experimentation and presenting only the most reasonable explanations. As you construct your report you will gain a better understanding of what actually happened in your experiment and why.

Finally, your instructor will use your reports to evaluate your learning. The grade you earn should reflect your understanding of the chemistry, procedures, techniques, and equipment used in the experiment.

While it is true that this is not a course in English composition, the credibility of the arguments you make in your reports will depend on the quality of your writing. The following situations are presented for your consideration. They pose problems not only for students, but also for scientists trying to have their work published. Keep them in mind when you write your reports.

Succinct sentences. Well-constructed sentences are succinct. They are easy to read and understand. And they make the most memorable statements. While it is true that a series of such sentences can make for boring reading, the most important comments should be presented in such sentences. For example:

> *"Unknown #96344 had two components. Component A was determined to be 1,4-dichlorobenzene. Component B was determined to be copper chloride."*

—vs—

> *"The organic component of the mixture could have been either propionamide or 1,4-dichlorobenzene, depending on how the data is analyzed, while the inorganic component of the mixture was probably copper chloride."*

Paragraphs. Long, run-on paragraphs are hard to read. Concise, succinct thoughts can usually be presented in paragraphs of three sentences or less. Make it difficult for your reader to get lost.

Tangible noun subjects. The key to writing a succinct sentence is to select the proper subject for that sentence. Whenever possible, use a tangible noun as the subject of the sentence. A tangible noun represents something that is touchable or concrete. They immediately direct the reader to the focus of the sentence. For example:

> *"A 50-milliliter beaker was used to catch the filtrate during the gravity filtration process."*

—vs—

> *"The procedure was performed so that the liquid came through the filter paper and was collected in a 50 mL beaker."*

Subject-verb location and agreement. Be careful placing modifiers between the subject and verb. The greater the distance, the more difficult it will be to understand the meaning. Keep your readers on track by placing the subject and verb as close together as possible. In addition, the subject and verb must agree in number (singular vs. plural forms) to avoid confusing the reader. For example:

> "Gravity filtration is the technique which will be used to achieve the separation of the two-component mixture by making use of the chemical property, solubility."

—vs—

> "Gravity filtration, which has an apparatus including a ring stand, ring clamp, pipestem triangle, funnel, filter paper, and beaker, and is based on the property of solubility, will be used to separate component A from component B."

Active/passive voice and first person. Although the active voice is more succinct than the passive voice, many scientists (and publications) prefer the latter. They believe the passive voice is more objective and, therefore, more suitable for scientific writing. In addition, the use of the first person can easily seem overly egocentric. In general, you should use the passive voice and avoid first person unless your constructions become too cumbersome. It is more important to be clear and succinct than to exclusively use the passive voice. For example:

> "Component A of Unknown #96458 contained dimethylaminobenzaldehyde. This was determined by melting point range and % carbon analysis."

—vs—

> "We figured out that A was probably dimethylaminobenzaldehyde, but we weren't sure because the temperatures weren't the same as the lab manual gives. My TA said that my component A had 49% carbon, but I couldn't get it to match up very well to anything. The dimethylaminobenzaldehyde seemed kind of close, so I chose that."

Wordiness. Excessive words may bog down the reader. Modifiers that don't enhance the content or meaning should not be used. Prepositional phrases often add unnecessary words. Evaluate such phrases to see if they can be recast as adjectives or adverbs.

Verb tense. Many writers are confused about when to use present tense and when to use past tense. The rules are simple.

1. Use present tense to describe experiments and data that already exist in the literature.

2. Use past tense to describe the experiments and data of the current report.

Composing your report. To present a convincing argument, your writing must be succinct and well organized. You should plan on writing at least two drafts. It is recommended that the first draft be in outline form. Word processors are an excellent aid for this kind of writing. You start by putting down your thoughts in the form of short phrases as they occur to you. Usually, this is most productively done while analyzing the data and observations and while reviewing the background information. This collection of thoughts can then be arranged into a coherent order. Finally, the phrases are crafted into complete sentences and paragraphs that easily and logically flow.

3-4 THE SCIENCE WRITING HEURISTIC

The Science Writing Heuristic, SWH, is a method that has been devised to encourage you to use hands-on guided inquiry laboratory activities to actively negotiate meaning and construct conceptual knowledge. Inquiry tasks, when correctly designed, stimulate your thinking about the underlying concepts related to the laboratory. The "answer" is not obvious from the outset.

The SWH provides an alternate format for you to guide your peer discussions and your thinking about and writing about how hands-on guided inquiry activities relate to your own prior knowledge via beginning questions, claims and evidence, and final reflections (Table 3-1). Although making observations in the SWH format may be similar to traditional verification work, the process of making claims and supporting them with evidence helps you to construct a deeper understanding of the concept(s) being explored by the laboratory exercise. Data collected via experimentation may be interpreted in more than one way. You must collaborate to construct possible explanations for what has been observed. Reflection on how your knowledge has changed helps you to confront possible misconceptions and construct a deeper, more appropriate understanding of the topic(s) being investigated.

Your learning environment is important. The Science Writing Heuristic requires an effective student-centered learning environment. The more you are able to make decisions, the more ownership, responsibility, and accountability you feel toward the laboratory exercise. You become more engaged—you exert more effort, are more interested in the outcome, and learn more as a result.

Table 3-2 outlines some differences between a traditional laboratory and a Science Writing Heuristic laboratory. A Science Writing Heuristic classroom is consistent with any other classroom employing an active learning strategy that promotes collaboration. You are responsible to one another to complete all necessary tasks, record your data and observations appropriately on the chalkboard for all to share, and attempt to formulate claims based on the evidence collected. The ensuing discussions help you and your classmates to connect your experimental work with related chemistry ideas, constructing your own understanding of the concept(s) under consideration.

We will use a specific format for the laboratory report that requires you to write. We do not use a fill-in-the-blank style report.

Table 3-1. Comparing student report formats for the Science Writing Heuristic and traditional laboratory.

The Science Writing Heuristic	
Standard Report Format	SWH Student Template
1. Title, purpose.	1. Beginning Questions—What are my questions?
2. Outline of procedure.	2. Tests—What do I do?
3. Data and observations.	3. Observations—What can I see?
4. Discussion.	4. Claims—What can I claim?
5. Balanced equations, calculations, graphs.	5. Evidence—How do I know? Why am I making these claims?
	6. How do my ideas compare with other ideas?
	7. How have my ideas changed?

Table 3-2. Comparing a traditional laboratory session to a student-centered laboratory session.

	Traditional Lab	Student-centered Lab
Pre-lab	The instructor gives step-by-step directions, asks for questions related to "cookbook" procedure.	a. Students write beginning questions (BQs) on chalkboard. b. Together the class discusses which BQs to investigate. c. Students talk about how to divide the tasks among groups, and what data needs to be collected. d. Students prepare class data table on chalkboard.
Students Perform Experimental Work	Students follow procedure outlined in lab manual or outlined by instructor. Students stay at their own experimental work station and talk mainly with their partner (unless they ask the instructor a question).	a. Students perform lab work necessary to answer their own questions. b. Students talk with other group members and other lab groups about what they are finding.
Data Collection	Lab partners check with one another to be certain that both have all data, then leave.	a. Each group enters data in class data table on the chalkboard. b. Groups who have finished "their" part walk around the classroom to check with other groups to determine whether any other group needs help in completing their task(s) or calculations.
Discussion	Student may ask a question of partner and/or instructor, then leaves the classroom.	a. As soon as more than half of the data has been entered in the table, students begin to look for trends to answer their BQs. If data does not agree with an apparent trend, they may repeat their work. b. When all data is on the board, students critically evaluate the information. c. Students work together to negotiate meaning, construct a concept, answer BQs. d. Students write and discuss an appropriate claim and provide supporting evidence.

3-5 SUMMARY OF THE SCIENCE WRITING HEURISTIC

The Process of the Science Writing Heuristic

Beginning Questions

a. Propose a beginning question to explore the purpose for doing the experiment.

b. A beginning question should be of the form "How does one variable depend on another variable?"

c. Beginning questions that are not acceptable include:

1. "Why?" questions.

2. Factoid questions.

3. Questions that can be answered without doing the experiment.

d. Can you make a prediction to try to answer your beginning question?

Safety Considerations

a. List what safety concerns should be considered when working with specific chemicals, equipment, or procedures in the laboratory.

Procedure and Tests

a. Propose your plan for how the beginning questions can be answered by doing the experiment. (This may be different from what you actually do during the experiment, but it is a start.)

b. Make an outline of precisely what you did (after sharing ideas with your group and drafting a group strategy). It should be written so that anyone could repeat the experiment exactly as it is written in the laboratory notebook.

Data, Observations, Calculations, and Graphs

a. List all data, observations, and notes that you and your classmates compiled during the experiment. Show how all calculations were performed.

b. This is a qualitative and quantitative summary of the experiment.

c. It includes data tables, balanced equations, mathematical equations, calculations, and graphs.

Claim(s)

a.   Make a statement about the results of your experiment to answer your beginning question(s).

b.   Do not merely repeat an observation.

Evidence and Analysis

a.   Write an explanation to support your claim(s).

b.   Refer to specific pieces of your own data, the class data, or both to explain your claim.

c.   Interpret or explain the information provided by specific data tables, chemical equations, calculations, or graphs.

d.   Explain any anomalies and what you did to repeat the work or incorporate the information with the rest of the data.

Reading, Reflection, and Post-laboratory Questions

a.   Discuss your initial question.

   1.   Have you explored

      a.   How your ideas have changed?

      b.   What new questions you have?

      c.   What new things you have to think about?

      d.   How your results compared to those of your classmates?

      e.   If you made a prediction prior to performing the experiment, was it correct? If not, do you understand why not?

   2.   How have you identified and explained sources of error and assumptions made during the experiment?

b.   Have you related this experimental work to concepts about which you have learned in class?

c.   To what can you refer in your text, notes, or some real-life application?

d.   How have you incorporated your answers to any post-laboratory questions into your reflection?

How Students Should Conduct Themselves in an Inquiry Laboratory

Student Guidelines for the Science Writing Heuristic and Inquiry Laboratories

Because inquiry-based laboratories are student-centered, you will be responsible for how you design your experiments and how you collect and analyze your data. Your instructor will serve as a guide or coach to help you to be successful. We have provided a suggested outline of what your responsibilities are during the process of the SWH.

1. Prior to arrival in lab

   a. Prepare beginning question(s), BQs;

   b. Outline a procedural strategy;

   c. List safety concerns.

2. Upon arrival in lab

   a. Write BQs on chalkboard while students are storing coats, book bags, etc.;

   b. Discuss BQs with partner or group mates;

   c. Discuss BQs with class to decide which one(s) to study as a group.

3. After deciding on BQ(s), discuss what strategies would be appropriate to answer the BQs.

   a. Divide class into groups (usually four or five people who can then subdivide into teams of two or three) to experimentally study all aspects of the BQ(s). All team members are expected to be working on some kind of laboratory procedure. No one should just watch!

   b. Each team member will need to understand how to conduct all parts of the laboratory. Eventually, when working the same kind of experimental procedures for the laboratory practical examination, each team member will be responsible to know what to do for each experiment.

   c. Be certain to provide for appropriate replication of procedures to create a large pool of "good" data.

   d. On the chalkboard, draft appropriate data collection tables, including dependent and independent variables to be investigated.

   e. Identify by initials which student groups or pairs are responsible for different runs. In this way, anyone can talk with the persons who collected any piece(s) of data.

4. After data has been collected, analyze it to try to interpret it.

    a. Look for trends, patterns, and anomalies.

    b. If there are anomalies, decide who will repeat the experiment to replace that data. How do you decide which part(s) to repeat?

    c. It is often useful to graph results and interpret your graph.

5. While waiting for all students to complete work and enter data, propose your claim(s), and cite supporting evidence.

6. Discuss results as class to create an understanding of the concept(s) for the lab. Your instructor will help to guide your discussion.

7. After lab,

    a. Consult other appropriate resources to explain, confirm, or dispute what you have learned in the laboratory. These could be your text, another reference text, the Internet, your instructor, your class notes, etc.

    b. Answer any "Post-laboratory discussion questions" that have been posed by your instructor or proposed in your laboratory manual.

3-6   SWH FORMAT-DETAILED

One of the most important components of your laboratory experience is your laboratory notebook. It is designed so that as you write, a carbonless copy is made on the next page. In this way, you can provide a copy of your work for your instructor to evaluate, while at the same time keeping a copy for yourself. It is in this notebook that you will prepare your pre-laboratory work (beginning question(s), safety discussion, and the draft of a procedure), draft the experimental procedure you actually follow during the laboratory period, record observations, compile data tables, prepare graphs, show calculations, state claims, list supporting evidence, and provide reflections on your work. Do not use another notebook or scratch sheets of paper. You can use your laboratory notebook as reference during the laboratory practical examinations.

Beginning Questions

After reading about the laboratory activity, write a question or two that can be answered by doing the experiment. Often the questions are in the form of a quantitative relationship. Sometimes the questions are qualitative in nature. Acceptable examples are: How does the temperature affect the rate of a reaction? How does the mass of the reactants affect the mass of product obtained? Unacceptable examples are: What is the limiting reagent? What color is my product? "Why" questions cannot be answered by doing the lab experiment and are considered nonproductive. For example: Why do we use a buret? Questions regarding procedure are not useful. An example would be: How do I set up a vacuum filtration apparatus? Students will need to share data in order to answer a question that has a relationship. For example: How does the amount of the limiting reagent affect the percent yield? Even though a question may seem obvious, it is important to ask that question, make a claim about it, and then back up the claim with evidence. After you propose a beginning question, can you make a prediction to try to answer it?

Safety

After reading the lab, list the major safety concerns for the lab experiment you are about to do. Additions can be made to your safety section during the pre-lab lecture. For example, you can list using gloves when appropriate, using the fume hood when producing a toxic gas, and appropriately disposing of waste products.

Experimental: Tests and Procedure

After reading the lab, list the steps that you will take to perform the laboratory experiment. You may have multiple sections. Keep in mind that a list of the major procedural steps written in your notebook may be useful on the lab practical, the laboratory "exam" that you will take in this course. What would you want to include if someone were going to use only your written procedure to do the lab?

After you and your group have agreed on a strategy for completing the experiment, outline that procedure if it differs from your own. You should list exactly what you did to accomplish your work.

Suppose that you are investigating the rate at which aluminum metal dissolves in hydrochloric acid. An appropriate procedure for a kinetics experiment might include:

1. Obtain a sample of aluminum between 0.50000 and 1.0000 grams.

2. Record the time (in seconds) necessary to dissolve the metal sample in 20.00 mL of hydrochloric acid with concentration ranging from 1.50 to 3.00 M.

Data: Observations, Graphs, and Balanced Equations

During the laboratory, enter all data, observations, notes, equations, graphs, chemical information, etc. into your lab notebook.

Calculations:

Sometimes you will need to mathematically manipulate your data in order to obtain a meaningful result. It is important to indicate how such manipulations were performed. One example of each type of calculation should be given. If the experiment requires the repeated use of the same calculation, give only one example using the first set of numbers. Each example should consist of three parts:

a. **The formula** that describes the calculation. An algebraic expression is preferred, but a written description of the operation will do.

b. **The formula in use.** Give the same formula, but with all the variables replaced with numerical values (except, of course, for the variable being determined).

c. **The answer.** Show the numerical value obtained from the calculation. Make sure that the answer has the proper units and correct number of significant figures. Remember: No number is correct unless it is properly labeled. Intermediate computations are not required as long as the above format is followed.

EXAMPLE: Determination of density.

$$\text{density} = \frac{\text{mass}}{\text{volume}} = \frac{114.6 \text{ g}}{26.72 \text{ mL}} = 4.287 \frac{\text{g}}{\text{mL}}$$

Claims

This is to be a one- or two-sentence statement about the results of your laboratory work that answers your beginning question(s). For example, an appropriate claim would be: If the concentration of reagent A doubles, so does the rate of the reaction. The reaction is first-order with respect to reagent A. An inappropriate claim would be: My product was a yellow solution.

Evidence and Analysis

This is a written explanation that supports your claims. How do you know that the rate of the reaction increases as the concentration increases? Include time vs. concentration data. Explain the meaning behind the data and calculations. Graphs, balanced equations, and calculations need to be interpreted and explained in order to count as evidence. Simply referring to them is not enough. Appropriate balanced chemical equations and necessary mathematical calculations can be used to support your claims, but the emphasis is on the interpretation and explanation of these results. Appropriate evidence for the claim that a reaction is first order with respect to reagent A is: When the concentration of reagent A doubles, the rate of the reaction doubles. When the concentration of reagent A is cut in half, the rate of reaction is halved. Rate = $k[A]^1$.

Reading, Reflections, and Post-laboratory Questions

Discuss your initial beginning question(s). Have your ideas changed? Do you have a new question? If you made a prediction prior to performing the experiment, was it correct? If not, do you understand why not? For example, "I thought that when you double the concentration of a reactant and that makes the rate of the reaction double that is a second order process. But, I have learned that when doubling the concentration of a reactant causes the rate to double, that is a first order process. For a second order process, doubling the concentration of a reactant should quadruple the rate of the reaction."

How do your results compare to those of students in other groups or the textbook or a literature value? Can you relate your work to any real-life application? What connections did you make between the lab and lecture? How have you incorporated your answers to any post-laboratory questions into your reflection?

3-7 SWH FORMAT—QUICK REFERENCE

Sections to Be Completed Prior to the Laboratory

Beginning Questions—What will I investigate?

Safety—How will I stay safe?

Tests and Procedure—What will I do to answer my question?

Sections to Be Completed in Lab

Data—Observations, Graphs, Balanced Equations, and Calculations—What did I see and what did I do? What calculations did I perform and how did I do them? What graph(s) did I prepare?

Sections to Be Completed Following Experimental Work but Before Leaving the Laboratory

Claims—How can I answer my beginning question(s)? What can I claim?

Evidence and Analysis—How do I know? Why am I making these claims? Provide written explanations that support claims.

Section to Be Completed in Lab (if possible) or After the Lab Period is Over

Discussion—Reading, Reflections, and Post-laboratory Questions—How have my ideas changed? Do I have a new question? How do my ideas compare with the ideas of others in the class? How will I answer post-laboratory questions?

3-8 LITERATURE-STYLE REPORT WRITING—OVERVIEW

Keep in mind that a lab report is a formal scientific argument. Each part of the report serves a function in making that argument. For the purposes of this course, we define eight parts to the report. The following description will begin with a brief summary of each part followed by more detailed explanations.

Title Page. Provides administrative information (author, date, etc.).

Abstract. A succinct description of the report content.

Introduction. A description of what is already known, the plan of action and expected outcomes.

Procedures. A description of the materials and techniques used in the experiment.

Results. An organized presentation of the observations and calculated results. This section is frequently dominated by figures, tables, and graphs. It will contain little or no text.

Conclusions and Discussion. Analysis of the data and presentation of conclusions regarding the original hypothesis. This should include a defense of the conclusions citing the results and a discussion of the reliability of the data used.

Appendixes. The next two sections are not normally part of a scientific paper, but will be included in your reports for educational purposes.

Raw Data and Observations. All notebook entries containing all measurements and descriptions made in the lab. Don't forget that this requires a date, your signature, and the signature of the instructor who supervised your work.

Calculations. Examples of all calculations performed to manipulate the numerical data. Include one example for each type.

3-9 LITERATURE-STYLE REPORT WRITING—DETAILS

Title Page

In a scientific paper, this page provides pertinent information such as the title of the article, the author, the publication, date of publication, location work was performed, etc.

For your reports, most of this information should be entered into your lab notebook before going to class. It can then be entered into a word processor for use in the report you submit.

- ◆ Title of experiment

- ◆ Report author's name (that's you)

- ◆ Names of any co-investigators (lab partners)

- ◆ Supervisor's name (lab instructor)

- ◆ Sponsoring organization (course and section number)

- ◆ Date(s) experimental work was performed

- ◆ Date the report was submitted

The format is up to you as long as the data is easily recognizable and interpretable. The only other thing to appear on the title page of the report is the **abstract**.

Abstract

An abstract is a brief summary of the important findings presented in the report. Only values and methods crucial to understanding the outcome are mentioned. Few, if any, details are included.

Abstracts are like those short blurbs generated by internet search engines that you get when you search for sites on a particular topic. They are used to find articles of interest to the reader. Because of the size of the body of scientific writing (thousands of journals), finding articles on particular topics is not easy. Abstracts must be short and succinct so they can be quickly digested.

Your abstract should be located on the bottom half of the title page. It is a brief summary of your important findings and should not exceed 75 words. Figure 3-3 is an example. Your abstract should not contain any introductory information. The names of procedures and techniques used should be mentioned but not described in any way. *It is strongly recommended that the abstract be the last thing you write.*

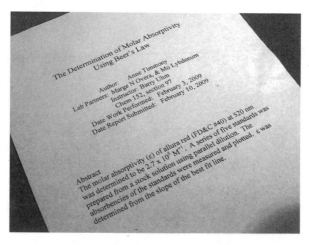

Figure 3-3. A title page and abstract.

Introduction

The following is a generic outline.

* Begin by stating the experimental objective. What is the experiment designed to achieve? Are any outcomes expected beforehand? If so, state them.

* Introduce the concepts and theories behind the experimental work to be performed. Argue that the experiment, based on known theory, should work.

* Finally, present all pertinent background information that bears on the experiment. It may be necessary to include physical constants and other properties.

A good introduction should not exceed three paragraphs and 200 words in length for a one-week experiment.

Procedures

This is your set of instructions for what you do in the lab. It includes descriptions of the materials, techniques, and procedures employed. The content will depend on what materials are provided for your use and the degree of detail in the procedures provided to you. Procedures printed in the lab manual should *not* be copied into this section. It is enough simply to reference them.

The procedure section is to be constructed before class and in your lab notebook. It should consist of a series of bullet points. Write on one half of the page, leaving the other half to write notes and comments as you perform the experiment.

Materials. Normally you will be provided with all the reagents and samples you will be using. In this case, a simple statement that all materials were provided by the preproom would suffice. Should you be required to provide any of your own samples to evaluate, this is where you would describe the source and how the samples were collected.

Reagents. Again, these are normally provided. Should you be required to prepare a reagent, this is where you would describe the procedure you used.

Techniques. If the procedures and techniques used in the experiment are provided in detail in the lab manual, a simple statement to this effect should suffice. If you are required to interpret the instructions or design your own procedures, here is where you will describe what you actually do in lab.

Results

This should be an objective and clear description of the experimental findings presented in a logical sequence that is easy for the reader to follow. In general, it is not appropriate to present conclusions. This section should include all raw data that was evaluated and any calculated results based on this data. It should be presented in a logical sequence that leads the reader to the conclusions to be presented later on. This means that the order in which the results are presented may not be the chronological order in which the data were collected.

This section is normally composed of charts, tables, and graphs and contains very little, if any, prose writing. Often a spreadsheet program like Excel is best suited for presenting some or all of the results. Descriptive observations should be presented as a series of statements that lead to, without stating, the final conclusion. Measurements should be organized into **tables** that also lead the reader through the various logical steps used to reach the final conclusion.

When it is possible to create **graphs** of raw data and calculated results, these should be included in this section. Sometimes observations are best represented with drawings rather than written descriptions. For example, when performing chromatography, drawings of the chromatograms are the easiest way to describe the results. All such representations of data are **figures** and should appear in this section.

Tables, graphs, and figures all must include a title, appropriate labels and well-defined boundaries. They are to be referred to by title in the conclusion section of the report.

Conclusions and Discussion

Here the author will discuss, interpret, and comment on the results. Conclusions must be justified by citing the pertinent background information and data obtained from the experiment. Limits placed on the conclusions by the quality of data collected and the nature of the techniques employed must also be discussed.

An important aspect of making a credible argument is demonstrating an understanding of other possible interpretations of the data. This section of a paper usually concludes with a discussion of additional experiments that could provide more and/or more accurate data that would either confirm or improve on the conclusions drawn.

The discussion should be organized as follows:

+ Present your conclusions, citing the observations that support them. Of course, the most important conclusion is the answer to your original hypothesis as set out in the introduction. Make sure this is clearly identified. Often it will be the first thing presented in the discussion.

+ When presenting your conclusions make sure you reference your tables, graphs, and figures as needed, including numerical results, descriptions of samples, etc. Make sure you describe the logic that was used to reach your conclusions. Why do they make sense?

* Discuss the quality of your data and the limits placed on your conclusions by the limits of the data you obtained. Discuss the limits placed on your conclusions by the techniques used. Sometimes data is only limited by the number of significant figures obtained. Other times the numbers may be considerably less reliable than the number of significant figures recorded. For example, if a sample was wet when weighed, how did this affect the calculated percent yield? If you suspect mistakes were made, describe them and the effect you believe they had on the data. If you believe equipment or reagent problems may have affected your results, describe how and in what manner.

* Based on your results, suggest additional experiments that could be performed to improve the quality of the conclusions presented. For example, if your measurements were not sufficiently precise, you might recommend performing more trials to see if greater precision is possible. If you obtained a negative result, you might suggest using a more accurate technique. If your conclusion is limited by the quantity and nature of the samples collected, you might recommend obtaining more samples.

* Finally, you will discuss any conceptual issues posed by the problem. You may also be required to make projections. Your instructor will provide specific direction on these points.

Appendices

The following two sections, while not parts of a normal scientific paper, are necessary for your instructor to properly evaluate your learning.

Raw Data and Observations

This section will be copies of all descriptions and measurements recorded in your notebook. While these would not be included in a journal article, your instructor will need them to help evaluate your experiment. Make sure the date, your signature, and the instructor's initials at the end are clearly discernable.

Calculations

Often it is necessary to mathematically manipulate the data in order to obtain a meaningful result. It is important to indicate how such manipulations were performed. Usually descriptions of the mathematical manipulations are included in the results section, although practice varies from field to field. Because this is an introductory course, you are being asked to present evidence of your data manipulations in a separate section. The actual calculated **values** should be presented in the results section along with the raw data. If there are no calculations, then this section will be omitted.

One example of each type of calculation should be given in this section. If the experiment requires the repeated use of the same calculation, give only one example using the first set of numbers. Each example should consist of three parts:

a. **The formula that describes the calculation.** An algebraic expression is preferred, but a written description of the operation will do.

b. **The formula in use.** Give the same formula, but with all the variables replaced with numerical values (except, of course, for the variable being determined).

c. **The answer.** Show the numerical value obtained from the calculation. Make sure that the answer has the proper units and correct number of significant figures. Remember: No number is correct unless it is properly labeled. Intermediate computations are not required as long as the above format is followed.

EXAMPLE: Determination of density.

$$\text{density} = \frac{\text{mass}}{\text{volume}} = \frac{114.6 \text{ g}}{26.72 \text{ mL}} = 4.287 \frac{\text{g}}{\text{mL}}$$

3-10 SUMMARY OF LITERATURE-STYLE REPORT CONSTRUCTION

Title Page

To include:

+   Title of experiment

+   Report author's name (that's you)

+   Names of any co-investigators (lab partners)

+   Supervisor's name (lab instructor)

+   Sponsoring organization (course and section number)

+   Date(s) experimental work was performed

+   Date the report was submitted

Abstract

75 words or less. A succinct description of the experimental outcomes.

Introduction

A description of:

* the experimental objective(s)

* pertinent background information

* expected outcomes, if any

Procedures

A description of the materials and techniques used in the experiment. For those procedures not in the lab manual, written procedures must be included.

Results

An organized presentation of the observations and calculated results made during the course of the experiment. This section frequently includes figures, drawings, tables, and graphs.

Discussion

Analysis of the data and presentation of conclusions regarding the original hypothesis. This should include a defense of the conclusions citing the results and a discussion of the reliability of the data used.

Appendices

Raw Data and Observations
All notebook entries containing all measurements and descriptions made in the lab. Don't forget that this requires a date, your signature and the signature of the instructor who supervised your work.

Calculations
Examples of all calculations performed to manipulate the numerical data. Include one example for each type.

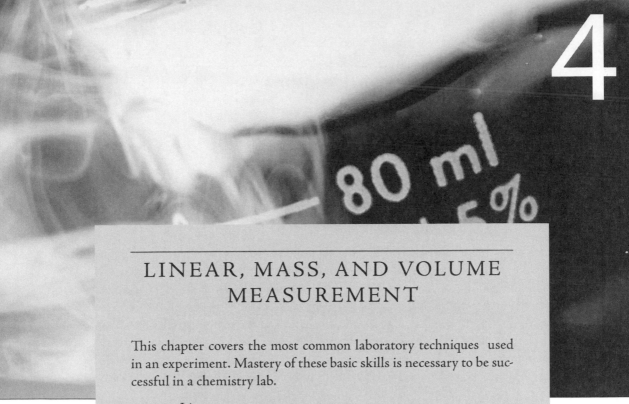

4

LINEAR, MASS, AND VOLUME MEASUREMENT

This chapter covers the most common laboratory techniques used in an experiment. Mastery of these basic skills is necessary to be successful in a chemistry lab.

+ Linear measurement.

+ Mass measurement.

+ Volumetric measurement.

Prior to the 17th century, chemical discoveries were based on observations of phenomena. Measurement was a crude and little used tool. By the early 1700s, though, careful measurement had become an accepted experimental tool and rather quickly led to the development of modern chemical theories. Today, precise measuring devices are an integral part of both research and applied science. The correct interpretation of experiments requires both precise measurements and an understanding of the error associated with those measurements.

4-1 LINEAR MEASUREMENTS

The term "linear" refers to one dimension. A linear measurement is the measurement of the length of an object in one dimension. Linear measurements made in two dimensions allow for the determination of area and in three dimensions yield volume. The most common tool for measuring length is a ruler and you are probably quite familiar with its use. What you may not be familiar with is making and recording values that accurately reflect the accuracy of the measurement.

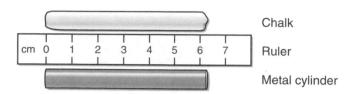

Figure 4-1. Linear measurements.

Consider the piece of chalk shown in Figure 4-1. Due to the irregular ends, the best reading is that the chalk is 6 cm long. Now consider the metal cylinder. It is more regular and we can more accurately read its length. In fact, we can estimate the distance between the marks on the ruler and come up with a more accurate reading. It is right and proper to read the length of the metal cylinder as 6.3 cm even though the ruler is marked only in centimeters. Such approximation is common in science and expected when using measuring devices. In this case, the edge of the cylinder is estimated to be 3/10 of the way between the 6 and 7 cm marks.

Vernier Caliper

A caliper is a device designed to accurately measure linear dimensions of irregular objects. It consists of two jaws fixed onto a ruler (see Figure 4-2). The jaws are brought together against the object to be measured. Most calipers have two sets of jaws—one for measuring outside diameters and one for measuring inside dimensions.

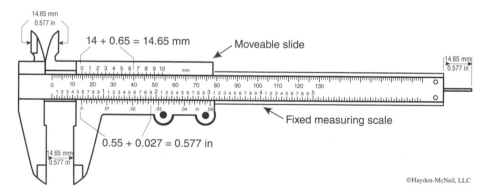

©Hayden-McNeil, LLC

Figure 4-2. A vernier caliper.

A vernier caliper is a caliper with a vernier scale attached. The vernier scale provides a more accurate way to measure the distance between two closely spaced marks. The vernier scale, located on the movable jaw, has marks that are 9/10 of the distance of the marks on the fixed scale. To read a vernier caliper you align the jaws on the object to be measured and read the fixed scale at the 0 mark on the vernier scale. If the 0 mark is not exactly over a mark on the fixed scale, you read the lower value off the fixed scale and then locate the mark on the vernier scale that lines up with one of the marks on the fixed scale. This becomes the next value beyond the value read off the fixed scale. Consider the example illustrated in Figure 4-3. The reading is 160.4.

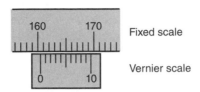

Figure 4-3. Reading a vernier scale.

4-2 MASS MEASUREMENT

In a chemistry lab, the mass of an object is determined by **massing** with a **balance**. If little or no accuracy is required, this is a rather trivial procedure. If a great deal of accuracy is required, it can be quite complicated. The following is a list of some issues to consider when trying to accurately mass an object.

+   **A wet object is heavier than a dry object.** For example, a damp beaker can easily weigh 0.01 g more than a dry one. In addition, the weight of a damp object will change with time as the water evaporates. If you place an object on a balance and notice that the weight continually drops, there is a good chance the object is wet. This could limit the accuracy of the measurement to 0.01 g or less, depending on the amount of water present.

+   **A dirty object is heavier than a clean object.** 0.001 g of dirt is not much dirt. For lab purposes, dirt is any unaccounted-for material such as dust, old labels, pieces of glass, grease, etc. Even visually small amounts of dirt can be a real problem if the object is weighed more than once. Dirt that comes off the object between weighings will adversely affect results.

+   **Fingerprints have weight.** Fingerprints can weigh 0.001 g. Getting fingerprints on objects will invalidate the weighing at the 0.001 g level and must be avoided for accurate weighings.

+   **Hot items.** Objects weigh less at higher temperatures. Even a moderately warm sample can weigh 0.001 g less than at room temperature. This is because the object heats the air above it, reducing the density of that air. The balance is zeroed against the room temperature air above the pan. The hot air weighs less and upsets this balance.

EXPLANATION OF TERMINOLOGY

The terms "mass" and "weight" have different meanings, yet are often used interchangeably in a chemistry lab. Mass is a property of matter and is the term used to describe the amount of matter in an object. Weight is the force exerted by an object in a gravitational field. As long as the gravitational field is constant, mass and weight are directly proportional.

A balance is a device that compares the mass of an unknown object with the known mass of another object (or set of objects). Ironically, these known masses are referred to as "weights." A scale is a device that measures the force exerted by an object due to gravity; in other words, its weight. Over time, the use of these terms has become very confused. It is common practice to say that "the weight of the beaker was determined to be 123.52 g." Technically, if the measurement was made on a balance, it would be more correct to say "the mass of the beaker was determined to be 123.52 g." Likewise, laboratory instructions often direct you to "weigh" objects. It would be more correct to direct you to "mass" the object.

All of this is admittedly very confusing. It is also not relevant to working in a chemistry lab. For the experiments you perform in this course, you can assume that the measured weights of samples are equivalent to their masses for evaluation purposes. When you are asked to "weigh" an object, you are to determine its mass using the available balance or scale.

The balance itself must also be considered. The reliability of the balance will depend on its cleanliness. Dirt and chemicals that get inside will have unpredictable effects. Chemicals, in particular, can react with the balance, causing corrosion and reducing its life span. To ensure that our balances give you reliable weighings and to preserve them for future students, the following rules govern the use of balances.

+ **Balances should not be moved.** If you feel the urge to do so, consult a lab instructor. Every time a balance is moved it needs to be recalibrated.

+ **Nothing but glass or metal objects should ever be placed on the surface of a balance.** Chemicals must never come in contact with the balance pan or any other part of the balance. For this reason, most of the weighing you do will be **weighing by difference.** In this technique, a container (beaker, weighing paper) is first weighed and then the material is added and the weight measured again. The weight of the material is the difference between the two weights.

+ **The balance should be cleaned after use.** Chemical spills must be cleaned up immediately. If you suspect that chemicals got inside the balance, report it to an instructor so that the balance can be properly cleaned.

Weighing a solid object that holds its shape (e.g., a beaker) is straightforward. The object is placed on the balance pan and the weight measured. Other situations may be more complicated. Here are some of the more common ones.

+ **Weighing chemicals.** Since chemicals must not be put directly on the balance pan, weighing by difference must be employed. Weighing paper is used to weigh chemicals that will be transferred to another container. This is a plastic-coated paper that chemicals will not adhere to. After weighing, the entire mass can be slid into a container. First the paper is weighed. Then the paper and chemical are weighed. The weight of the paper is subtracted to obtain the weight of the chemical. Some balances allow you to **tare** a container. To tare is to adjust the balance to read zero with the container on it. Electronic balances can be tared with the push of a button.

 Another suitable container is a beaker or flask. If the chemical is to be used in a beaker or flask, it is best to make the weighing directly in the container. First weigh the container, then add the chemical and weigh again. The weight of the container is subtracted to obtain the weight of the chemical. Again, it may be possible to tare the balance with the container on the pan.

+ **Weighing liquids.** The problem is similar to that of weighing a solid chemical. The solution is the same. Weigh an empty, dry container. Add the liquid and weigh again. Subtract the weight of the container to get the weight of the liquid.

+ **Weighing by subtraction.** Sometimes we're not sure how much of a chemical we'll be using, but we still want an exact weighing. Weighing by subtraction addresses this problem. The maximal amount of chemical is estimated. A container is prepared with this amount of chemical plus a little extra. The container and chemical are weighed. Chemical is removed and used as needed. When done, the beaker and left over chemical are weighed. The difference is the weight of chemical used.

Procedure for Weighing with an Electronic Analytical Balance

A more accurate device is the **electronic analytical balance.** It is capable of measuring mass to the nearest milligram (.001 gram) or less. It is quick and reliable. It is also expensive and sensitive. It operates by measuring force. The pan is connected to a metal ribbon in such a way that a weight on the pan is mechanically translated into a torque on the ribbon. A stepping motor is also attached to the ribbon. The balance measures the voltage that must be applied to the motor to just balance the torque on the ribbon. This voltage is then electronically converted to a mass value that is displayed.

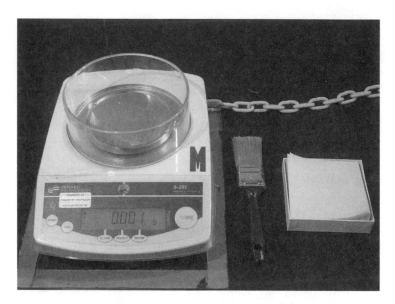

Figure 4-4. An electronic balance.

Because there are no moving parts, the balance is less sensitive to motion and shock than other balances. Because of the electronics, it is very sensitive to chemicals, particularly liquids and gases (fumes). Chemical spills can easily destroy one of these balances.

The balance is operated with control buttons. Different models have different arrangements. There are two controls you need to identify to use a balance. One is the **ON-OFF** button. The other is the zero control. This will usually be labeled as **zero, re-zero, tare,** or **0/T**. Its function is to set the scale display to 0 g when there is nothing on it.

Figure 4-5. Balance control panel.

Using the Balance

1. Check the pan to see if it is clean and dry. If not, clean it and dry it. If the balance has doors, close them.

2. If the balance is off, press the ON/OFF button. The balance will go through a self-calibration procedure that will last a minute or so. Wait for the display to fill with zeros.

3. Press the TARE button. Again wait for the display to fill with zeros.

4. Place the object to be weighed on the pan.

5. Wait for the display to stop changing, then read and record the value.

6. Remove the object. Clean the pan and surroundings. Leave the balance ON unless instructed otherwise.

4-3 VOLUMETRIC MEASUREMENTS

Volumetric measuring devices are very common in our world. Most kitchens have measuring cups and spoons. A volumetric measuring device is any container that will contain a known volume when filled to the mark. When making a volumetric measurement, there are two issues that determine how accurate the measurement will be. One is the accuracy with which the device was calibrated when it was made. Molded plastic and glass containers will only be as accurate as the machines that make them. The more accurate the device, the more expensive it will be. Common kinds of laboratory volumetric devices and their accuracies will be discussed below.

The other issue is determining when the surface of the liquid is at the mark. When a water solution is poured into a glass container, it "wets" the sides of the container. The resulting curved surface is known as a **meniscus**. All volumetric glassware is designed to be read at the **bottom** of the meniscus. When reading the meniscus make sure your eye is level with the meniscus.

When reading volumetric glassware, you should always estimate the value to one more significant figure than the smallest marks on the device. In the example pictured in Figure 4-6, the bottom of the meniscus falls between the marks for 88 mL and 89 mL. By visually proportioning the position of the meniscus between the two marks, the value of 88.6 mL is obtained.

When measuring a specific volume of solution, add solution to the container until the bottom of the meniscus just touches the appropriate mark. In this case the volume is read to one more significant figure than the mark. For example, if the bottom of the meniscus in Figure 4-6 had been just touching the 88 mL mark, the volume would be read as 88.0 mL.

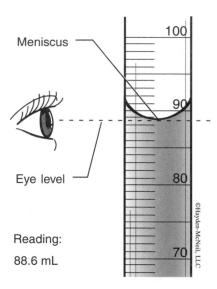

Figure 4-6. Reading the meniscus.

4-4 VOLUMETRIC DEVICES

The following are brief descriptions of the various devices available to you in the lab.

Beakers and Erlenmeyer Flasks

These are designed to hold solutions and not for making measurements. The accuracy of the markings on a beaker is usually only ±10%. Beakers and flasks can be used for approximating volumes when accuracy is not required.

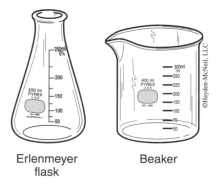

Figure 4-7. Erlenmeyer flask and beaker.

Burets

A buret is a long, calibrated tube with a valve (called a "stopcock") on the bottom. Burets are designed to deliver a variable amount of solution to the nearest 0.01 mL when used properly. Some things to consider when using a buret are:

+ Operation of the stopcock can be tricky and requires practice to do quickly and reliably. For starters, the buret should be held upright with a clamp leaving both hands free to work the stopcock. Hold the body of the stopcock with one hand while turning the valve with the other. With practice, you should be able to deliver single drops with a buret.

+ There is a dead volume at the bottom of most burets. If the liquid level falls below the last marking, an accurate reading will not be possible.

+ Before use, a buret should be rinsed with some of the solution that will fill it. This is to prevent dilution errors that will occur if the inside of the buret is wet.

+ All air must be removed from the buret. Any air present is volume that does not contain solution. This could very well lead to volume readings that are too large. There are two places where bubbles can be found. In the buret tube they tend to cling to the sides. Tapping the buret to dislodge them usually works. The other place is in the stopcock. After filling the buret, run solution through the stopcock until all air is removed.

+ If a drop of solution remains on the tip of the buret, its volume will be measured but not delivered. There should be no drops of solution on the tip at the start or at the end of the measurement.

+ It is considered bad form to try to fill a buret to a particular volume. The action of trying to exactly fill it could bias your results. Instead, you should fill the buret then read the volume.

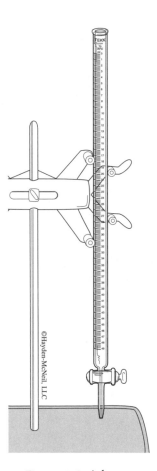

Figure 4-8. A buret.

♦   The position of the meniscus in a buret can sometimes be difficult to read. One thing that helps is to draw a straight, dark line on a white piece of paper (an index card is ideal). This is held behind the buret with the black line behind the meniscus. The white background and reference line should help you read the volume in the buret.

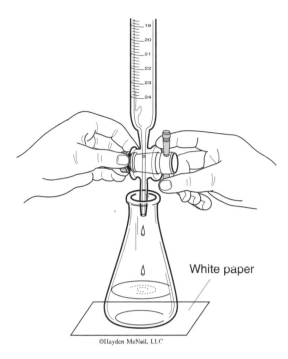

Figure 4-9. Manipulating the stopcock.

Eyedroppers

These are small glass or plastic tubes designed to deliver very small volumes of solutions. They come with detachable rubber bulbs. Although they have no markings, they can be calibrated and used for volumetric measurements. To calibrate an eyedropper, count the number of drops required to add 1.00 mL of water to a small graduated cylinder. An eyedropper normally has a drop volume of about 0.05 mL. The rubber bulbs have a limited lifetime. As they age they get hard and brittle. Eventually they will need replacement.

Micropipets

These can be either glass or plastic. The glass ones are like eyedroppers in that they have detachable rubber bulbs. A glass micropipet normally has a very long, thin snout (for getting into test tubes) and a drop volume of about 0.03 mL. The plastic ones are usually one molded piece of plastic. Sometimes they will have markings on the sides that allow for one significant figure measurements.

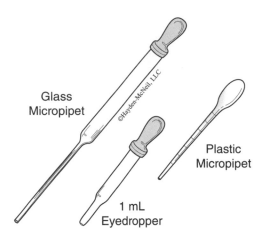

Figure 4-10. Eyedropper and micropipets.

Graduated Cylinders

A glass cylinder with calibrated volume markings on the side designed to measure the volume of liquid contained. The accuracy depends on its size. For small graduated cylinders is usually 0.1 mL.

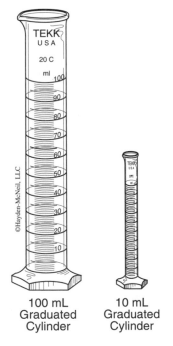

Figure 4-11. Graduated cylinders.

Volumetric Pipets

A glass or plastic tube used to accurately deliver specific volumes. A volumetric pipet has only one mark on it. When filled to this mark, the pipet will contain the indicated volume to the nearest 0.01 mL.

Graduated Pipets

A glass tube with a series of volume markings. Solution is drawn up into the pipet with a pipet bulb to a level above the desired mark. The bulb is removed and the end covered with a finger. Solution is allowed to drain away until the meniscus is at the correct mark. The pipet is now positioned over the receiving vessel and solution allowed to drain until the desired volume has been delivered. The markings on a graduated pipet usually don't go all the way to the end. Thus, this kind of pipet will always have some solution remaining after use. Graduated pipets are designed to deliver solutions to the nearest 0.01 mL.

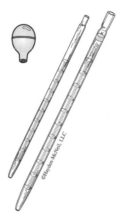

Figure 4-12. Graduated pipets.

How to use a pipet.

(applies to both volumetric and graduated pipets):

+   Rinse the pipet with a small amount of the solution to be measured.

+   Using a pipet bulb, draw solution up into the pipet to a level above the mark.

+   Remove the bulb and cover the end of the pipet with a finger (it usually helps to wet the finger to make a good seal). Roll the finger, allowing solution to drain away until the meniscus is at the mark.

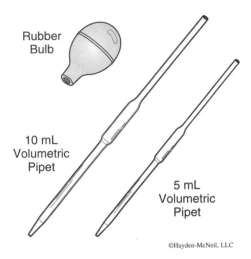

Rubber
Bulb

10 mL
Volumetric
Pipet

5 mL
Volumetric
Pipet

©Hayden-McNeil, LLC

Figure 4-13. Volumetric pipets.

✦   Position the pipet over the receiving container and allow the contents to drain.

There is a trick to using a pipet. When a pipet drains, a small amount of solution will remain in the pipet. Whether or not you leave this in the pipet depends on the design of the pipet. If it has a small **TD** printed on it, it is designed "**to deliver**" the specified volume. This means that a small amount of solution should remain in the pipet. Its volume was accounted for when the pipet was calibrated. The proper technique for using a TD pipet is to touch the tip to the inside of the receiving vessel, above the liquid surface, and allow the solution to drain down the inside of the vessel.

If the pipet has a small **TC** printed on it, it is designed "**to contain**" the specified volume. This means that the small amount of liquid remaining in the pipet is part of the measured volume. These are usually graduated pipets (see below) and require two readings (before and after). If the entire volume is to be used, all solution needs to be blown out of the pipet into the receiving vessel. Use the pipet bulb to do this.

If there is no marking on a pipet, you should assume it is designed **to deliver**.

Figure 4-14. Close-up of the markings on a "to deliver" pipet.

Volumetric Flasks

This flask has one mark on its neck. When filled to the mark, the flask contains its design volume to the nearest 0.01 mL. Notice that this is a "**to contain**" and not a "to deliver" device. This is the most accurate volumetric measuring device presented here.

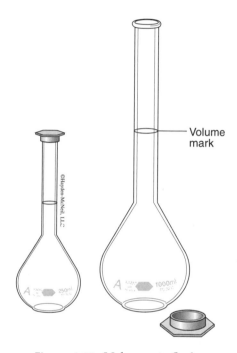

Figure 4-15. Volumetric flasks.

5

SEPARATION TECHNIQUES

This chapter presents four common laboratory techniques for separating chemical compounds.

+ The extraction of molecules having particular properties from larger collections.

+ The separation of solids from solution using filtration.

+ The separation of solids from solution using centrifugal force (centrifugation).

+ The selective precipitation of molecules from a solution (recrystallization).

5-1 SOLVENT EXTRACTION

A solvent is used to separate one or more molecules from a mixture. It is most commonly used with complex mixtures such as biological samples and soils. It can also be employed with complex chemical reactions to remove a desired product from the reaction mixture.

Extraction from Biological Samples

There are two issues to address when extracting substances from biological samples. One has to do with the structure of the sample. How will the solvent actually come in contact with the substances? Simply putting cells in a solvent does not guarantee the substances inside the cells will be extracted. The other is water. Biological samples contain water. The extraction process will likely release water. If the water is not wanted it needs to be removed. This will probably be the case if you are extracting with an organic solvent. For such solvents as ethanol, methanol, and acetone water will change the characteristics of the solvent and must be avoided.

Procedure for Biological Sample Extraction

a.   Determine if water will interfere with the extraction. If so, begin by drying the sample as much as possible. Do your best to avoid adding any water during the extraction procedure.

b.   Put a small amount of the dry sample in a mortar. It should be just enough to cover the bottom of the mortar.

c.   For plant materials, if the component to be extracted is inside cells an abrasive will be needed to break down the cell walls. A pinch or two of clean sand is ideal.

d.   Add a small amount of the solvent. It should be just enough to cover the sample.

©Hayden-McNeil, LLC

Figure 5-1. Mortar and pestle.

e.   Grind the sample until you are comfortable the cells have been sufficiently reduced.

f.   Decant the solvent into a small container and proceed.

Depending on the nature of your separation there are two other issues you may need to consider.

a.   When grinding biological materials, you will be releasing water. If you are using an immiscible organic solvent you may end up with two layers. If so, you may need to separate the layers. This is best done by placing the liquid in a small test tube and drawing one of the layers off with a transfer pipet (Figure 5-2).

b.   The volume of solvent used in the extraction may need to be reduced. Usually this is done to concentrate the extracted components. The best approach is to place the solution in a small beaker and put it on a hot plate with a very low setting. For organic solvents this must be done in a hood.

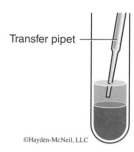

Transfer pipet

©Hayden-McNeil, LLC

Figure 5-2. Removing a layer.

5-2 FILTRATION

The separation of materials is one of the most common operations performed in a chemical experiment. The oldest, simplest, and cheapest method of separation is the filtration of a solid from a liquid. Many procedures are explicitly designed to take advantage of this technique.

A filtration is performed by passing a solid/liquid mixture through a membrane that retains the solid while allowing the liquid to pass through. The nature of the membrane is very important. The larger the pores in the membrane, the more quickly the filtration will proceed. But a large pore size will allow finely divided solid particles to pass through. A membrane with small pore size will retain the more finely divided solid material, but will take longer to use. Selection of the proper membrane is often a critical decision.

Items required for a filtration are a container for the original mixture, a funnel of some sort to hold the membrane, and a receiving vessel, often referred to as a filter flask. The most commonly used membrane is filter paper. This comes in different sizes, shapes, and pore-sizes. Paper is good to use, as the cellulose fibers create a matrix with many channels for the liquid to run through. One problem that often occurs is that a layer of the solid will build up on the surface of the paper and prevent the liquid phase from passing. This can be compensated for by physically moving the solid with a spatula, or allowing the solid to settle while still in the original container, and then **decanting** as much of the liquid through the filter paper as possible before allowing any of the solid to settle on the filter paper.

The key feature of any separation technique is the differential movement of the materials to be separated. In a filtration, the liquid phase is made to move while the solid material remains in place on the filter paper. The source of the movement is gravity. The liquid is poured on top of the filter paper, and gravity forces it through the paper. If gravity alone is the motive force, the filtration is referred to as a **gravity filtration**. Sometimes, however, gravity is insufficient. Perhaps more speed is needed. Or perhaps gravity alone is insufficient to force the liquid through the filter paper. Additional force can be generated by pulling the air out of the filter flask. In this case, the air pressure on top of the liquid in the filter funnel adds to the force of gravity in pushing the liquid through the filter paper. This second method is known as **vacuum filtration**.

General Description of Gravity Filtration

A **funnel** is secured over a receiving vessel, usually a beaker or flask. A convenient way to support the funnel is with a **clay triangle**, **ring** and **ring stand**. Figure 5-3 illustrates such an arrangement. A round piece of **filter paper** is folded into quarters, opened up and placed in the funnel. Note that the filter paper will not "sit" in the funnel until some of the solution has been used to wet it.

The solution to be filtered is poured into the center of the filter paper. It is usually a good idea to pour as much of the liquid as possible through the filter paper before getting too much solid into the filter funnel. The more solid in the funnel, the slower the filtration will go.

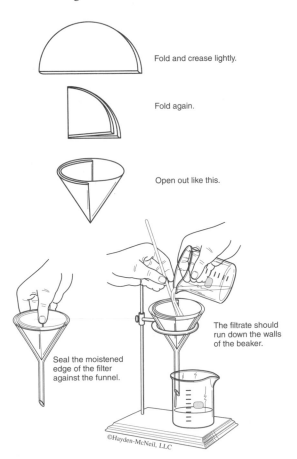

Fold and crease lightly.

Fold again.

Open out like this.

Seal the moistened edge of the filter against the funnel.

The filtrate should run down the walls of the beaker.

©Hayden-McNeil, LLC

Figure 5-3. Gravity filtration setup.

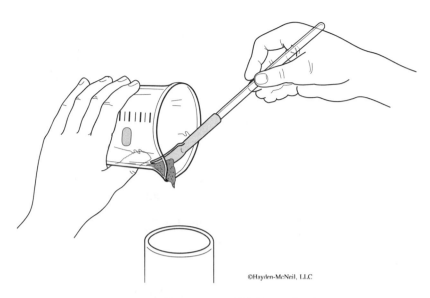

©Hayden-McNeil, LLC

Figure 5-4. Removing solid from a beaker.

When all liquid has been poured into the filter funnel, the remaining solid can be scraped from the original container into the filter funnel (Figure 5-4).

The more finely divided the solid is, the more it will slow down the filtration. One aid is to *flute* the filter paper. This will increase the surface area of the filter paper, allowing more liquid to pass. To flute a piece of filter paper, fold it into eighths. Open it up and fold it back and forth to create a corrugated effect (Figure 5-5). Note that it will not stay in the funnel until some weight has been added.

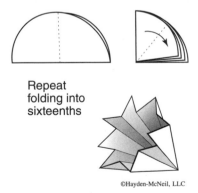

Repeat
folding into
sixteenths

©Hayden-McNeil, LLC

Figure 5-5. Fluted filter paper.

Funnels come in long-stem and short-stem. Long-stem funnels are usually preferred for water solutions. If the tip of the funnel is in contact with the solution in the receiving vessel, the rate of filtration will be faster. With volatile solvents like acetone, evaporation from the tip of the funnel could clog it up. Short-stem funnels are usually preferred with volatile solvents.

If either the filtered solid or the **filtrate** (what passes through the funnel) is to be quantified, caution must be taken. Once all the solution has drained from the funnel, some will still remain in the filter paper and the filtered solid. This is removed by **washing** the filtered solid with one or more small portions of fresh solvent.

Outline of Gravity Filtration Procedure

+ Assemble filtration setup.

+ Fold filter paper and place in funnel.

+ Pour liquid through filter paper, collecting the filtrate.

+ Transfer solid from original container into the filter funnel.

+ Wash the filtered solid with pure solvent.

General Description of Vacuum Filtration

A vacuum filtration apparatus is assembled as shown in Figure 5-6. It consists of a specialized funnel known as a **Büchner funnel**, a **side-arm flask**, and a length of **vacuum tubing**. When the funnel is placed into the flask, the tip of the funnel should point away from the side-arm. This is to prevent the filtrate from being sucked out of the flask. The tubing is used to connect the flask to a vacuum source such as a vacuum pump or a vacuum outlet. The assembled apparatus is usually unstable. It is a good idea to secure the flask to a ring stand with a clamp.

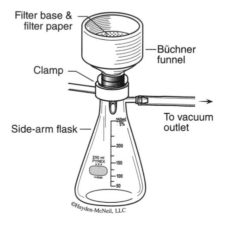

Figure 5-6. Vacuum filtration setup.

A piece of filter paper of the correct size is placed into the Büchner funnel. A few drops of the solvent to be used are added to "wet" the filter paper and help it seat in the funnel. If this isn't done, the filter paper may float when the solution to be filtered is added, allowing solid to pass through.

The vacuum is turned on and the solution is poured into the center of the filter paper. The strength of the vacuum pull is adjusted to produce a good flow rate. One problem that can occur here is the lifting of the filter paper caused by liquid getting underneath it from the sides. A spatula or glass rod can be used to hold the paper down until sufficient material is on top of it to hold it down.

Once all the solution has drained from the funnel, some of it will still remain in the filter paper and the filtered solid. If either the filtered solid or the filtrate is to be quantified, the filtered solid must be washed. This is done by pouring small portions of fresh solvent onto the solid. The best way to add the solvent is with an eyedropper, micropipet, or wash bottle. One of the advantages of a vacuum filtration is that the suction pulls more of the solvent from the solid and filter paper. Thus, wash volumes are usually much smaller for vacuum filtrations than for gravity filtrations.

The vacuum can also be used to air dry the solid in the funnel. This is done by continuing to draw air through the funnel while stirring the solid with a spatula. The dry air passing through the funnel will remove by evaporation the remaining solvent in the filtered solid. It is a good idea to loosely cover the funnel with a larger piece of filter paper or ribbed watch glass. This is to prevent dust and dirt from contaminating your solid. Remember that the air you are pulling through the funnel comes from out of the room. It needs to be filtered.

If the solvent is not water, it probably will be necessary to use a trap between the filter flask and vacuum outlet. A trap is a flask inserted into the vacuum line that is designed to trap unwanted chemicals. For example, the trap could be a flask placed into an ice bath to condense solvent fumes. Another kind of trap is one arranged so that the gas coming from the filter flask passes through a solution. This is a good way to remove acidic or basic gases such as nitrogen oxides or ammonia.

The major disadvantage of a vacuum filtration relative to a gravity filtration is that the filter paper has a much smaller effective surface area. This means that it is much easier to plug up the filter paper in a vacuum filtration. A spatula is often used to move the solid around to prevent the paper from plugging up. For very finely divided solids, gravity filtration may be better.

5-3 CENTRIFUGATION

The centrifuge is a device that uses centrifugal force to separate materials of different densities. It is most commonly used to separate solids from liquids. It consists of a rotor attached to an electric motor. Samples are placed in holders attached to the rotor and spun around by the motor. To prevent vibration, the centrifuge is balanced by placing equal masses of sample on each side of the rotor. Vibration will keep the sample mixed up and cause undue wear on the centrifuge.

The centrifuges available for your use require two matched tubes to operate. The ideal tubes are plastic centrifuge tubes designed specifically for this purpose (Figure 5-7). If centrifuge tubes are not available or not suitable for the particular use, select two test tubes that are the same size, diameter, and weight.

With your sample in one, add water to the other until the volumes are the same. This second tube is your balance tube. Place your sample in one holder and the balance tube in the holder exactly opposite. If others are using the same centrifuge, make sure your test tubes are labeled!

Figure 5-7. Centrifuge tubes.

Figure 5-8. A desktop centrifuge.

Turn the centrifuge on for about one minute, then turn it off. Allow the rotor a few minutes to slow down and stop on its own. DO NOT attempt to slow down the rotor with your hands. It is DANGEROUS!

Removing test tubes from the centrifuge can be tricky if they do not protrude from the holder. In this case use forceps to grasp the lip of the test tube and slide it out. Don't forget your balance tube.

Finally, you will need to remove the solution (known as the supernatant) from the centrifuge tube without disturbing the solid at the bottom. Pouring off the liquid could disturb the solid causing a re-mixing of the components. The best way to remove the liquid is with a transfer pipet (Figure 5-9).

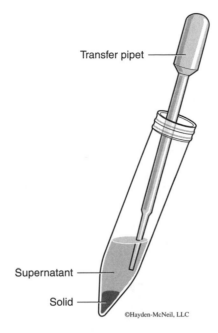

Transfer pipet ───

Supernatant ───

Solid ───

©Hayden-McNeil, LLC

Figure 5-9. Removing the supernatant.

5-4 RECRYSTALLIZATION

Recrystallization relies on the different solubilities of your desired product and the impurities included in the reaction mixture. The *impurities* may be unreacted reactants or other undesired products (*by-products*).

When recrystallizing it is important to select an appropriate solvent. This will be one that, when hot, will dissolve the desired product and the impurities, yet, when the solvent cools, only the impurities will remain dissolved and the "pure" product will crystallize out of solution. At that point, the crystals can be easily separated from the impurities using a filtration technique.

1. Prepare an ice-bath slurry.

2. Put a small amount of the recrystallizing solvent in a beaker and heat to boiling on a hot plate. Note that the hot plate should be set on a LOW setting. *As soon as the solvent begins to boil, remove it from the hot plate.*

3. Put the crude material in a small beaker. Using an eyedropper, add the hot solvent to the crude product, one drop at a time and with constant mixing, until all solid has dissolved. It may be necessary to warm the beaker on the hot plate to keep the solvent warm. Immediately set the beaker in the ice bath to cool. Do this in such a manner that the ice water does not get into the beaker. If crystals have not begun to form after five minutes, ask your instructor

to demonstrate how to promote their formation. Leave the beaker in the ice bath for at least ten minutes after crystals begin to form.

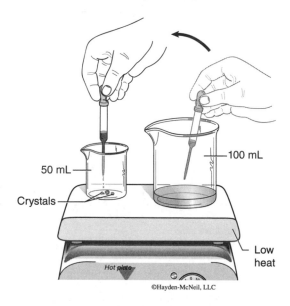

Figure 5-10. Dissolving product in hot solvent.

4. Use the vacuum filtration apparatus to separate the crystals from the solvent. For this filtration, use cold solvent to wash your crystals. Once again, use your spatula to transfer the crystals; do not add any more liquid to the beaker or funnel.

5. Continue to draw air through the crystals until they are dry. When dry, you can determine their weight.

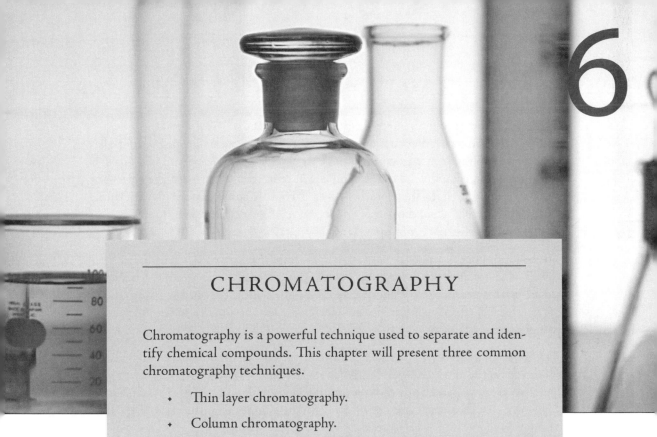

CHROMATOGRAPHY

Chromatography is a powerful technique used to separate and identify chemical compounds. This chapter will present three common chromatography techniques.

+ Thin layer chromatography.

+ Column chromatography.

+ Ion-exchange chromatography.

The key to chromatography is movement. The idea is to take a mixture of materials to be separated and cause them to move along a path in such a way that each chemical species moves at a different rate. Thus, after a period of time, each species will have moved a different distance and will therefore be separated from the others.

Differential movement is achieved by the differential interactions of the substances to be separated with two phases: the mobile phase and the stationary phase. An effective chromatography requires the selection of phases with suitable interactions to achieve separation. Interactions can be based on chemical or physical properties. Movement can be achieved by such things as gravity, capillary attraction, or gas pressure. The variety of interaction and movement options results in many different kinds of chromatography.

6-1 THIN LAYER CHROMATOGRAPHY

Thin layer chromatography (TLC) is a rather quick and cheap technique for separating small amounts of material. It is usually used to identify the components of a mixture. Because it only works well with small amounts, and due to the difficulty retrieving the separated components, it is not usually used to obtain pure, separated materials.

TLC uses a solvent to move materials along a solid support. Most often the movement is achieved by capillary action. The mixture to be separated is placed on the support and solvent caused to move across the sample. As the solvent moves past the sample, the components of the sample will tend to interact with the solvent and move along with it. The more strongly a particular substance reacts with the solvent, the further along the path it will move. A substance that does not interact at all with the solvent will not move at all.

The solid support is usually a glass, plastic or metal plate covered with silica (silicon dioxide) or alumina (aluminum oxide). The material to be separated is dissolved in an appropriate solvent and spotted onto the bottom of the plate. The bottom edge of the plate is put into contact with a solvent and the solvent allowed to move across the plate.

TLC is particularly useful for identifications due to the property known as the **retention factor** (or retardation factor or rate factor), abbreviated R_f. As the chromatography progresses both the solvent and the sample will move up the plate. While the distances each travels will be constantly increasing, the ratio of those distances will always be the same.

$$R_f = \frac{distance\ sample\ moves}{distance\ solvent\ moves} \tag{6-1}$$

For the same sample using the same solvent and the same support the retention factor will always be the same. An unknown compound can be identified by performing a TLC and comparing the R_f to either a known run simultaneously or reliable literature values.

Performing Thin Layer Chromatography

1. Obtain a suitable chromatography plate. Keep it clean and dry and avoid handling it with your hands. Water, dirt, and fingerprints could cause the plate to behave in an irregular manner.

2. Select a suitable developing chamber. If the developing solvent is volatile (and it usually is) the chamber needs to be closed. This is most conveniently done using plastic wrap.

3. Obtain the designated developing solvent and put some in the developing chamber. The desired amount should fill the chamber to a depth of a bit less than 1 cm. Cover the chamber and allow it to sit while you prepare the plate. The idea is to allow the air in the chamber to become saturated with solvent vapor.

4. Take the plate and identify the place you intend to spot your sample. It should be close to one end, but far enough along the plate so that when the plate is placed in the solvent the spot will *not* be covered with solvent. A bit more than 1 cm should do it.

5. Spot your sample onto the plate. A small-diameter capillary tube is often the best tool to use. The spot should be as small and as concentrated as possible. This is best achieved by putting a small spot on the plate, allowing the solvent to dry from the plate, then repeating the spotting procedure again, applying the second spot to exactly the same place as the first.

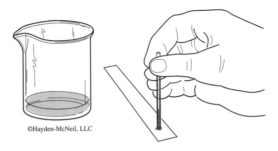

©Hayden-McNeil, LLC

Figure 6-1. Spotting a TLC plate.

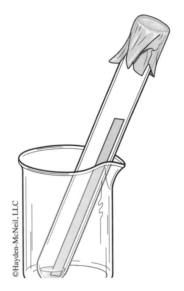

©Hayden-McNeil, LLC

Figure 6-2. Developing a TLC plate.

NOTE

Capillary tubes are GLASS WASTE. Make sure they ultimately end up in the designated glass waste container.

6. Put the plate in the developing chamber (spotted end down) taking care to see that the solvent does not slop onto the plate. Cover the chamber.

7. Allow the chamber to sit undisturbed while the solvent moves up the plate. In most cases this will be 10 to 20 minutes.

8. Remove the plate when the solvent is about 1 cm from the top edge. Immediately make a pencil mark at the solvent front and allow the plate to dry.

9. Identify the sample spots and mark them. It is always a good idea to draw pictures of the plates. It is also quite possible you will not be able to see the sample spots. If so, you will have to perform another procedure to make them visible.

10. UV viewing. Many organic substances are visible in ultraviolet light. If a suitable UV lamp is available you can illuminate the plate to make the spots visible.

11. Iodine chamber. Iodine will react with many organic substances to produce colored compounds. Place the plate in the iodine chamber and seal it. Shake the chamber to get some of the iodine dust on the plate. Leave the plate in the chamber for a few minutes. Remove it and mark the spots.

12. Clean up. Deposit glass-backed plates in the glass waste. Put plastic-backed plates in the solid chemical waste bucket. Put all the solvent solutions in the liquid waste bucket. Put capillary tubes in the glass waste.

NOTE

The different solvent mixtures may travel at different rates. Different strips may finish at different times.

6-2 COLUMN CHROMATOGRAPHY

Another method is to put the solid support in a container and pour the solvent on top, allowing gravity to move the solvent down through the support material. This technique is known as **column chromatography** because it is usually performed in a glass or plastic column. Like TLC, it is a rather cheap and easy technique to perform. But unlike TLC it can be used to collect the separated components for further experimentation or analysis.

A column open at both ends is packed with the appropriate solid support material. The column is then saturated with solvent and a steady stream of solvent passing through the column is established. Sample is introduced at the top of the column and the effluent (solvent coming out the bottom of the column) is monitored for the presence of sample components. The more strongly the components interact with the solid support the slower the material will move through the column. The more strongly the components interact with the solvent the faster the material will move through the column. The effluent is collected at the appropriate times.

There are some tricks to running a good column. The column must have some kind of porous plug at the bottom to prevent the solid support from leaking out. The support material must not be packed so tight that the solvent will run too slow through the column. The column must not be allowed to run dry. The sample must be introduced onto the column in as concentrated a plug as possible to ensure it does not spread out too much as it passes through the column.

Building a Small Silica Column

1. Preparing the solid support (silica). Place a couple of grams of silica in a small beaker. Add roughly 15 mL of the appropriate solvent. Take a plastic transfer pipet and cut the end off (Figure 6-3). Use this to stir to create a slurry. The pipet will also be used to put the slurry into the column.

©Hayden-McNeil, LLC

Figure 6-3. Clipped transfer pipet.

2. Building the column. Obtain a short-stem glass micropipet. Take a small piece of cotton and insert it into the micropipet. Push it to the bottom of the pipet. A long-stem micropipet is a good tool to use (see Figure 6-4). This is to prevent the gel from running out of the bottom of the pipet. Stand the pipet up, point down, in a test tube. Fill the pipet half-full with solvent.

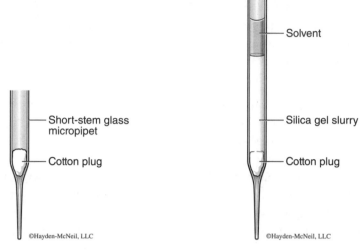

Figure 6-4. Cotton plug.   Figure 6-5. Completed silica gel column.

Using the transfer pipet add the silica gel slurry to the micropipet. Add small amounts at a time and allow the gel to pack into the column. Use more solvent as necessary to wash the gel down into the column. Adding the gel too fast will cause the gel to clump up and not pack properly. The solvent will run out the bottom of the micropipet and fill the test tube. Empty the solvent from the test tube as needed. Figure 6-5 pictures a completed column.

NOTE

You must continuously add solvent to the column to prevent it from running dry. Should you need to stop the solvent flow, put the pipet into a test tube full of solvent (see Figure 6-6). The flow will stop if the solvent level in the test tube is the same as the solvent level in the column.

3. Loading the sample. Use a long-stem glass micropipet to add the sample to your column. Try to avoid getting sample on the inside walls of the pipet. Allow the sample to soak into the gel (Figure 6-6). Using a clean transfer pipet, slowly add solvent to fill the pipet. Avoid disturbing the gel in the column.

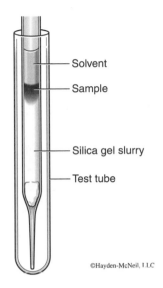

Solvent

Sample

Silica gel slurry

Test tube

©Hayden-McNeil, LLC

Figure 6-6. Column with sample.

4. Collecting the first component. Continue to add solvent and watch the effluent. When you notice the first component starting to come out of the pipet, move the pipet to a fresh test tube. Continue collecting until the component has finished draining out of the pipet. Move the column to another test tube.

5. Collecting more components. Repeat step 4 to collect additional components. It may be necessary to change the solvent to get more components to come off the column. If so, you want to make as sharp a distinction between the solvent layers as you can. Allow the solvent level to drop to the top of the gel and then carefully layer the new solvent on top.

NOTE

It may not be possible to remove all the components.

6. Clean up. Deposit the used silica gel in the solid chemical waste bucket. Put all the solvent solutions in the liquid waste bucket. Put the micropipet in the glass waste.

6-3 ION-EXCHANGE CHROMATOGRAPHY

Ion-exchange chromatography is a special kind of column chromatography. Unlike the chromatography described above, the solid support material is capable of reversibly binding certain kinds of ions. It depends on a material known as an *ion-exchange resin*, which is a material, usually a synthetic polymer, that can be made into large beads. The surface of the bead is chemically modified so that it is capable of involvement in equilibrium reactions. For example, ion-exchange resins take advantage of acid–base equilibria. The resin contains covalently bound weak acids or bases whose equilibria govern the exchange. There are two kinds of ion-exchange resins that use acid–base equilibria: *cation-exchange resins* and *anion-exchange resins.*

A *cation-exchange resin* has many weak acid molecules attached to the resin. Usually, these are high valence sulfur compounds. The weak acid protons can be displaced by cations in a reversible reaction where M^+ represents any monovalent positive ion and R refers to the polymer body of the resin.

When a solution is in contact with the resin, the equilibrium will be established. Cations with a charge greater than one can also displace protons, but since charge must be conserved, they will occupy a number of sites on the resin equal to the size of their charge.

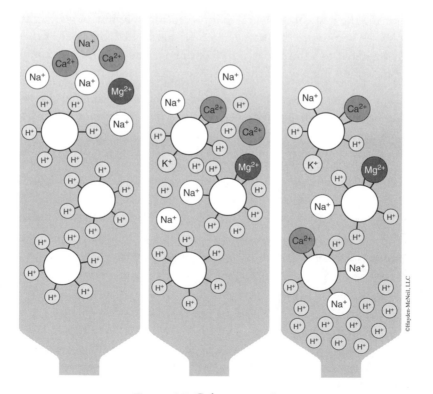

Figure 6-7. Column reactions.

Consider what happens if a sample high in cations is introduced to the top of a column containing such a resin. As the solution percolates down the column the cations will be "exchanged" for hydronium ions as the high $[M^+]$ drives the reaction to the right (remember Le Châtelier's Principle) until equilibrium is reestablished. This process occurs continuously as the sample progresses down the column. The solution that comes out the bottom of the column will contain essentially no cations except hydronium. The amount of hydronium ion will be equal to the total number of positive charges present in the original sample (a divalent metal ion, e.g., Mg^{+2}, will react in a balanced manner and release two protons).

After samples have been run, the resin can be regenerated by running a moderately concentrated acid through the column. Now the high $[H_3O^+]$ will cause the reaction of Equation 6-2 to proceed to the left to reestablish equilibrium. Again this will occur continuously down the column so that essentially all the positive ions, except the hydronium bound to the resin, will pass out the bottom of the column. All cationic sites on the resin will be protonated.

$$R-\underset{\underset{O}{\|}}{\overset{\overset{O}{\|}}{S}}-O-H \; + \; M^+ \; \rightleftharpoons \; R-\underset{\underset{O}{\|}}{\overset{\overset{O}{\|}}{S}}-O-M \; + \; H^+ \tag{6-2}$$

$$\left(R-\underset{\underset{O}{\|}}{\overset{\overset{O}{\|}}{S}}-O-H\right)_n \; + \; M^{+n} \; \rightleftharpoons \; \left(R-\underset{\underset{O}{\|}}{\overset{\overset{O}{\|}}{S}}-O\right)_n M \; + \; n\,H^+ \tag{6-3}$$

Ion-exchange resins can also be made to exchange anions. In this case, quaternary ammonium salts are usually used (6-4).

$$\left(R-\underset{\underset{R}{|}}{\overset{\overset{R}{|}}{\overset{\oplus}{N}}}-R \; OH^{\ominus}\right)_n \; + \; A^{-n} \; \rightleftharpoons \; \left(R-\underset{\underset{R}{|}}{\overset{\overset{R}{|}}{\overset{\oplus}{N}}}-R\right)_n A^{-n} \; + \; n\,OH^- \tag{6-4}$$

Ion-exchange resins are the heart of a rather common water softening technique. Deionized water is made by passing water first through a cation-exchange resin then an anion-exchange resin. The cations are exchanged for hydronium ions and the anions for hydroxide ions. The hydronium and hydroxide combine to form water leaving a solution containing no ions except the hydronium and hydroxide normally present due to the dissociation of water. (Of course, deionized water does not remain that way for long as it absorbs oxides of carbon, nitrogen, and sulfur from the air.)

Exchange resins can be made that take advantage of other equilibria. One recent development of interest is the attachment of antibodies to resins. The antibodies, being very specific, will remove only certain molecules from the sample solutions. The use of antibodies does have one drawback. Most antibodies attach molecules so strongly it is difficult to get them to release them after removing them from solution.

As Equation 6-3 above states, when a sample is loaded onto the cation exchange column, one hydronium ion will be released for every positive charge (PC) in the sample. Thus, the governing equation for the cation exchange will be

$$\text{moles PC in sample} = \text{moles } H_3O^+ \text{ released from the column} \qquad (6\text{-}5)$$

Once the sample has been loaded on the column, it can be washed through the column and collected from the bottom. Note that the released ions do not "magically" appear at the bottom of the column. They are released into the water surrounding the resin. To be detected, they must be physically moved through the column and into some other container for further testing. This is done by pouring more water on top and "pushing" the sample out the bottom of the column where it is collected in an Erlenmeyer flask.

The total moles of released ion in the column effluent can be determined by an acid/base titration. You will remember that one mole of hydronium ion will be neutralized by one mole of hydroxide.

$$H_3O^+ + OH^- \rightleftharpoons 2\,H_2O \qquad (6\text{-}6)$$

and therefore at the endpoint (neutrality)

$$\text{moles } H_3O^+ = \text{moles } OH^- \qquad (6\text{-}7)$$

A pre-standardized solution is used to titrate samples to the bromothymol blue or phenolphthalein endpoint. For the cation exchange, which releases hydronium ion, a pre-standardized NaOH solution is best. Using equations 6-7 and 6-5, the moles of PC present in the sample can be calculated. The sample volume can then be employed to calculate the original [PC].

6-4 PERFORMING ION-EXCHANGE CHROMATOGRAPHY

The following procedure is for the performance of ion exchange chromatography using a cation exchange resin to determine the total positive charge in water samples.

Building a Column

Figure 6-8 is an illustration of an assembled column. If an assembled column is not available, you'll have to build one. Here's how. Obtain 50 mL of the resin from the reagent bench. Fill your squeeze bottle with deionized water. Secure your empty column to a ring stand using a buret clamp. Make sure the stopcock is closed.

Add some water to the beaker containing resin to create a slurry that will pour easily. Obtain a small piece of glass wool and loosely roll it into a ball. The uncompressed ball of glass wool should be about 2 cm in diameter. Flatten the ball into a disk and push it to the bottom of the column and hold it there. The next operation is rather tricky. Pour the resin into the column making sure the resin does not get under the glass wool. Resin that gets under the glass wool could plug up the stopcock.

CAUTION

The resin beads are like miniature marbles. They are very annoying and can cause problems if you get them on the floor or work surfaces. Be careful with them.

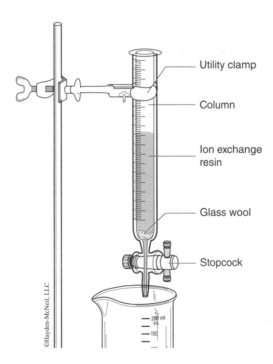

Figure 6-8. A cation exchange column.

Open the stopcock and allow the water to drain out of the column. As the water level drops, add water from your squeeze bottle (to the top of the column) to prevent the water level from dropping below the top of the resin. If air bubbles appear in the resin, stir it up to expel them. Once you are comfortable that the resin is well packed and the column flows freely (at least three drops per second), close the stopcock.

Chromatography

CAUTION

To avoid breaking the stopcock, make sure you hold the body with one hand while turning the valve with the other.

Column Regeneration

This procedure is required to ensure that all the binding sites are occupied by hydronium ions. Use a beaker (250 mL recommended) to collect waste solution. Open the stopcock at the bottom of the column and allow solution to drain out until the solution level in the column is exactly level with the top of the resin. Close the stopcock. (Note: now is a good time to practice controlling the rate of solution flow with the stopcock. It is recommended you add more water and practice until you are comfortable operating the equipment.)

Use your graduated cylinder to obtain 10 mL of the 3 M HCl regeneration solution. Carefully add the HCl to the column taking care to disturb the resin as little as possible. Open the stopcock and allow the solution level to again drop to the top of the resin. Carefully layer water (from your squeeze bottle) on top of the resin and fill the column to the top. Open the stopcock and allow solution to pass through (into your waste beaker) at a rapid rate. As the water level nears the top of the resin, add more. Continue until 100 mL of water has been added to the column.

Now you will check the pH of the effluent to see if all the excess regeneration solution has been washed through the column. Slow the column flow until it is dripping at a rate of less than one drop per second. Obtain a piece of pH paper and test the pH of distilled water. Now test the pH of the effluent. If it is different than distilled water, run another 20 mL of water through the column and check the pH again. Continue this process until the effluent has the same pH as the distilled water. Allow the water level to drop to the top of the resin and stop.

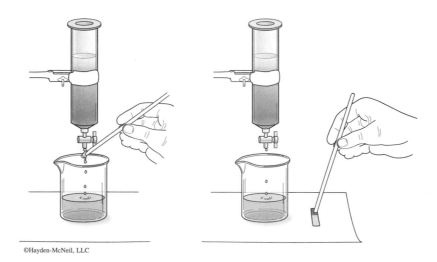

Figure 6-9. Checking effluent pH.

Loading a Sample onto the Regenerated Column

The recommended sample size is 10.00 mL for the first trial. You may want to adjust this size for future trials based on the outcome of the titration. A pipet is recommended for ease of adding sample to the column. Deposit your sample into the column. Open the screw clamp and allow the sample to percolate into the column until the solution level is even with the top of the resin. Again layer water on top of the resin without disturbing your sample solution. You will need at least 30 mL of distilled water to wash the sample through the column.

Now you will collect the sample in an Erlenmeyer flask. Care must be taken to avoid loss. Replace the waste beaker with a clean Erlenmeyer flask. Open the screw clamp and collect the effluent in the Erlenmeyer flask. This time it is important to control the flow rate to prevent the sample from becoming too spread out on the column. You should adjust the flow so that the effluent is dripping out at the rate of one to two drops per second. As the solution level in the column drops, add more distilled water. After 30 mL has been added, check the pH of the effluent. If it is not the same as distilled water, run another 10 mL of water through the column. When the pH of the effluent is the same as distilled water, replace the Erlenmeyer flask with the waste beaker and set the flask aside in a safe place. Allow the water level in the column to drop to the level of the resin.

Set the column aside and perform the titration. When done, determine the best sample size to produce a desired titration volume. Run at least three more samples through the column, collecting the effluent in different Erlenmeyer flasks.

Sample Titration

Titrate each sample separately using a standard strong acid/base titration procedure. This is discussed in Chapter 10-4. You will need a standardized solution of NaOH. The amount and concentration will depend on the cation concentration in your sample. For most applications, 100 mL of a 0.1 M solution should suffice.

7

SUBSTANCE CHARACTERIZATION

Phase changes are intensive physical properties that can be used as fingerprints to identify substances. Measurement of phase changes can also be a valuable indication of the purity of a sample, since impurities will cause the phase change to be lower than those of a pure sample. This chapter presents two common phase change measurements.

- Melting point determination.
- Boiling point determination.

7-1 MELTING POINT DETERMINATION

The melting point of a substance is an intensive property that is not changed by anything other than purity. For this reason it is commonly used as a tool for identifying pure substances. It is also useful for qualitatively determining the purity of a substance. The further the measured melting point of a sample is from that of the pure substance, the more impure the sample.

When a melting point is measured, a **melting point range** is obtained. For example, the accepted melting point range for acetylsalicylic acid is normally reported as 135–136°C. The first number is the temperature at which the solid just begins to melt. The second number is the temperature at which the last of the solid disappears.

If a sample is impure, the values will be lower and the range will be broader. This second point is particularly useful. The melting point range of a pure substance will normally not be greater than one or two degrees. A broader range is a strong indication that the sample is not pure.

The measuring of melting points requires having a thermometer in thermal equilibrium with the sample. If the thermometer is not at the same temperature as the sample the wrong values will be reported. This is best achieved if the sample is in direct contact with the thermometer. But it is also desirable to use as small a sample as possible. The most common way of measuring melting points has the sample placed in a very small glass tube known as a closed-end capillary tube (see Figure 7-1). The tube can then be secured adjacent to a thermometer and heated.

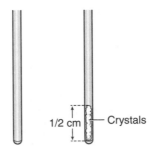

1/2 cm — Crystals

Figure 7-1. Capillary tubes.

Melting points are commonly measured using specially designed devices. Figure 7-2 illustrates such a device. Most work on the "hot block" principle. An electric current is used to heat a block of metal. A thermometer and a capillary tube containing sample are placed in holders that allow them to rest on the hot block. An eyepiece is provided to make it easier to view the sample. Power is applied until the sample melts.

Potential Problems

The biggest problem in using a melting point device is overheating the block. The power must be turned off as soon as possible after the sample melts to avoid this problem.

The measurement of melting points only works with stable compounds. Many compounds decompose before they reach their melting point. This can be deceiving as the decomposition may look like melting.

The presence of a solvent can also be a problem. If the material to be melted comes from a procedure involving solvent there is the distinct possibility that some solvent remains in the sample. This is true even if the sample appears to be dry. It is particularly true for samples obtained by recrystallization and samples obtained from water. What will happen is that at some point during the heating the sample will dissolve in the remaining solvent. This is easily mistaken for the melting of the solid creating an erroneous value.

Measuring Melting Point with a Mel-Temp Device

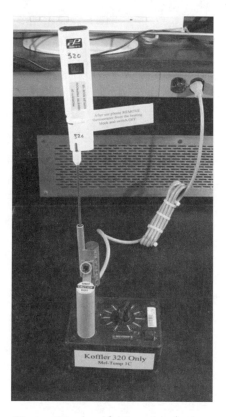

Figure 7-2. A melting point device.

1. Obtain a melting point capillary tube from the reagent bench (this should be a long capillary tube with one end sealed—see Figure 7-1).

2. Crush your product and put enough in a capillary tube to create a column about ½ cm in height. Pack the material using a long glass or plastic tube (Figure 7-3). Hold the long tube upright on the bench top and place your mp tube into the top of the tube. Drop your mp tube onto the bench. Repeat until the solid is appropriately packed into the capillary.

Figure 7-3. Packing the capillary.

3. Insert the capillary tube into the appropriate slot in the mel-temp. Look through the viewport to ensure you can see your sample (Figure 7-4).

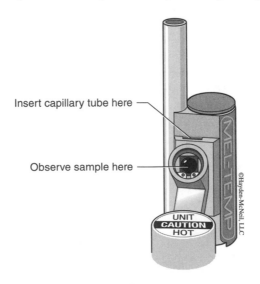

Figure 7-4. The viewport.

4. Turn the power up to begin heating the block. Do not heat the block too quickly. Watch the sample. As soon as the first particle melts, read and record the temperature in your notebook. Continue to watch the sample. As soon as the last particle melts, read and record the temperature. Immediately turn off the power. The two temperatures are your melting point range. If time permits, repeat this procedure to confirm your determination.

7-2 BOILING POINT DETERMINATION

The boiling point is the temperature at which a liquid becomes a gas. The temperature of a liquid can not, under normal conditions, rise above the boiling point. The temperature of a boiling liquid will remain at the boiling point until all the liquid has been converted to gas.

Boiling points are dependent on the pressure over the liquid phase. In order to compare measured boiling points with other measured or literature boiling points it is necessary to know the pressure over the liquid. Normally this is done by making sure the boiling liquid is open to the atmosphere. Then the pressure can be assumed to be the current atmospheric pressure.

Figure 7-5 illustrates the boiling point apparatus available for your use. It consists of a conical vial inserted in an aluminum hot block. On top of the vial is an adapter, a temperature probe, and a condenser. Sample is placed in the vial and the hot block heated with a hot plate. The thermometer is situated so that the sensing part of the probe is just above the surface of the liquid. The condenser is to minimize vapor loss from the system. As the vapor rises from the boiling liquid and enters the condenser it will condense back to the liquid phase and drain back into the vial.

NOTE

For a small amount of a sample with a relatively low boiling point, it will not be necessary to cool the condenser with water.

The temperature probe is connected to a Vernier Go!Link, which is in turn connected to a computer and operated with the Logger *Pro* software. The current temperature is displayed in a box. When the ▶Collect button is selected Logger *Pro* will begin recording the temperature every few seconds. The data will be displayed in the graph. The graph is the best way to monitor the temperature for a boiling point determination. As the liquid is heated the temperature will climb on the graph. When the liquid begins to boil the temperature will stop rising. This will be the boiling point.

Measuring a Boiling Point

1. Assemble a boiling point apparatus as illustrated in Figure 7-5.

2. Add liquid to the vial through the condenser. Add sufficient liquid to fill the vial about half full. A transfer pipet is suitable for most liquids. Make sure the temperature probe is positioned with the tip just above the surface of the liquid.

3. Confirm that the temperature probe is properly connected to the computer. Start the "Logger *Pro*" software. Make sure the temperature is actively displayed on the screen.

4. Turn on the hot plate. An initial setting of 5 is recommended. It is important to not overheat the hot block. If the block gets too hot the liquid will boil too vigorously preventing the temperature from being measured accurately. It will also be difficult to keep liquid in the apparatus.

5. In Logger *Pro* start data collection by selecting the ▶Collect button. Monitor the temperature. If it is climbing too fast reduce the heat. When the temperature trace begins to level off, turn the heat off. The plateau will be the boiling point temperature.

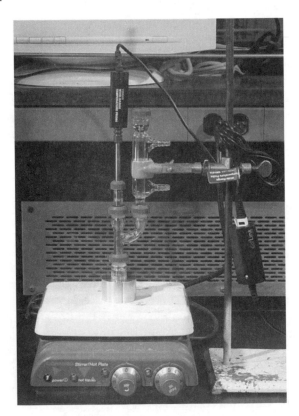

Figure 7-5. Boiling point apparatus.

8

SPECTROSCOPY

Spectroscopy is a powerful tool for counting atoms and molecules and observing how they behave. This chapter will present the more common aspects of spectroscopy.

+ Spectroscopy.

+ Spectrometers.

+ Emission spectroscopy.

+ Absorption spectroscopy.

One major problem with the study of things at the atomic level is that they are way too small to be seen even with the most powerful microscopes. While it is true that images have recently been made of individual atoms, the techniques used are very limited and not practical for most applications. Although we can't make images of atoms and molecules, we can use light to learn about them. This is because atoms and molecules can absorb and emit light. The technique for looking at such light is referred to as **spectroscopy**. It is the only tool available to astronomers to collect information about the universe outside our solar system. It is the most powerful tool available to scientists to study atoms and molecules and a technique that is universally used in science and engineering.

8-1 PROPERTIES OF LIGHT

Spectroscopy is the study of the interactions of light with matter. In common usage, the word **light** refers to what we see with our eyes. To a scientist, the term is the common name for all **electromagnetic radiation**. Light is energy transmitted through space that has characteristics of both particles and waves. All waves have a **wavelength**, the length of one complete cycle (Figure 8-1).

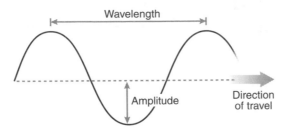

A. Longer wavelength, lower frequency

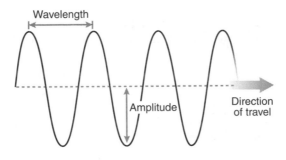

B. Shorter wavelength, higher frequency

©Hayden-McNeil, LLC

Figure 8-1. Wavelength.

For light, the range of possible wavelengths is infinite. For a long time, the different forms of electromagnetic radiation were believed to be different phenomena, because they interacted with matter in distinctly different ways. Thus, we have the collection of common names ending in -wave and -ray for the various wavelength ranges (microwave, x-ray, etc.). Figure 8-2 gives the range of known wavelengths of electromagnetic radiation and the common names given to radiation of particular wavelengths.

Theoretically, spectroscopy can be performed using light from anywhere in the electromagnetic spectrum. In reality, we are limited by the way the light interacts with matter and our ability to detect and measure light of particular wavelengths. The infrared, visible, and ultraviolet regions are the most useful in chemical laboratories. **Infrared spectroscopy** is particularly useful for studying the bonds between carbon, hydrogen, oxygen, and nitrogen atoms that predominate in organic compounds. Thus, infrared is a key tool of the organic chemist. Infrared spectra can indicate the presence of particular structures in unknown organic compounds by the presence of characteristic features. They can also be used to confirm the identity of compounds by comparison with known spectra. Reference books containing thousands of spectra of known organic compounds are available for this purpose.

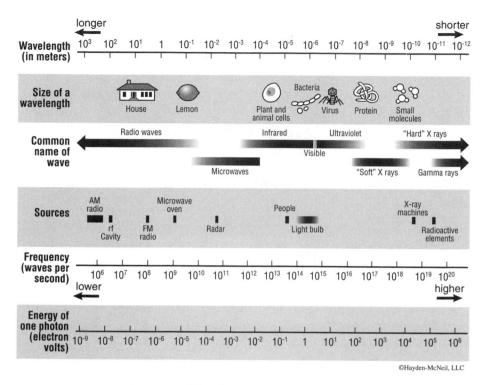

Figure 8-2. The electromagnetic spectrum.

Visible light spectroscopy is particularly useful for studying certain kinds of organic compounds and elements that have electrons in d-orbitals, such as transition metals. **Ultraviolet spectroscopy** is useful for studying certain kinds of organic compounds that predominate in biological contexts. All proteins have useful ultraviolet spectra as does DNA and many reaction co-factors. Many biochemical reactions can be effectively monitored in the ultraviolet and this tool is commonly found in biochemical laboratories. In clinical laboratories, ultraviolet spectroscopy is often the means for making quantitative determinations on plasma and urine samples.

8-2 KINDS OF SPECTROSCOPY

There are two distinct aspects of this interaction that can be used to learn about atoms and molecules. One is the identification of the wavelengths of light that interact with atoms and molecules. The other is the measurement of the amount of light being absorbed or emitted at any particular wavelength. Both determinations require separating a light source into its component wavelengths. Thus, a critical component of any spectroscopic measurement is the breaking up of light into a **spectrum**.

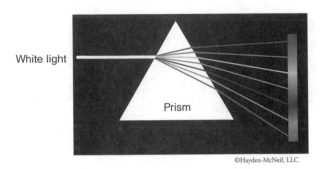

©Hayden-McNeil, LLC

Figure 8-3. Spreading the light.

For each of these aspects there are two ways observations can be made: the light that is **absorbed** by atoms and molecules, and the light that is **emitted**. This creates a total of four different kinds of spectroscopy.

Qualitative Spectroscopy. One of the useful aspects of spectroscopy derives from the fact that the spectrum of a chemical species is unique to that species. Identical atoms and molecules will always have the same spectra. Different species will have different spectra. Thus, the spectrum of a species can be thought of as a fingerprint for that species. **Qualitative spectroscopy** is used to identify chemical species by making a spectrum and comparing it with known spectra to find a match. Figure 8-4 shows the spectrum of an F-class star and the wavelengths that are indicative of certain elements.

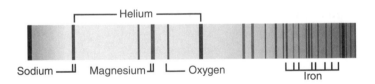

Figure 8-4. Stellar spectroscopy.

As an example, consider the discovery of the element helium. It was first observed not on earth, but in the sun! In 1868, the French astronomer, Pierre-Jules-César Janssen, was in India to observe a solar eclipse when he detected new lines in the solar spectrum. No element known at that time would produce these lines, and so he concluded that the sun contained a new element. This initiated a search for the new element on planet earth. By the end of that century, the new element had been identified in uranium ores and was named helium, after the Greek word for the sun, *helios*. Today, spectroscopy finds wide application in the identification of chemical species.

Quantitative spectroscopy is one of the quickest and easiest ways to determine how many atoms or molecules are present in a sample. This is because the interaction of light with matter is a stoichiometric interaction. At any given temperature, the same number of photons will always be absorbed or emitted by the same number of atoms or molecules in a given period of time. This makes spectroscopy one of the few techniques that can provide a direct measure of the number of atoms or molecules present in a sample.

Emission spectroscopy is the study of light emitted by atoms and molecules. The electrons of the sample are promoted to very high energy levels by any one of a variety of methods (e.g., electric discharge, heat, laser light, etc.). As these electrons return to lower levels they emit light. By collecting this light and passing it through a prism, it is separated into a spectrum. When viewing an emission spectrum, we will see only a dark field with colored lines that correspond to the electron transitions (see Figure 8-5). Notice that the absorption and emission spectra of the same substance will have the same values for wavelength. In the absorption spectrum these values will appear as black lines on a colored field, whereas in the emission spectrum they will be colored lines on a black field.

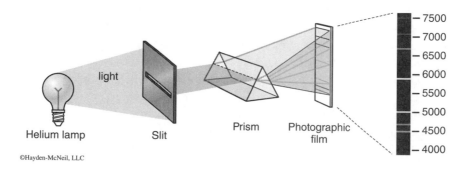

Figure 8-5. Helium emission spectrum.

Quantitative emission spectroscopy requires samples be heated very hot to enable electrons to emit light. Most often, this is done by feeding the sample into a burner flame. As a result, it is not practical for use with most molecular compounds. It is frequently employed for elemental analysis. A quantitative emission technique, flame photometry, is employed in clinical labs to determine sodium and potassium levels in blood plasma and urine.

Absorption spectroscopy is the study of light absorbed by molecules. In it, white light is caused to pass through a sample and then through a device (such as a prism) that breaks the light up into a spectrum. You will recall that white light is a mixture of all wavelengths of visible light. When such light is passed through a sample, under the right conditions, the electrons of the sample will absorb certain wavelengths of light. Thus, the light coming out of the prism will be missing those wavelengths. We will see a spectrum with black lines where the absorbed light would have been if it had not been removed by the sample. Figure 8-6 is a graphical representation of what a helium absorption spectrum would look like.

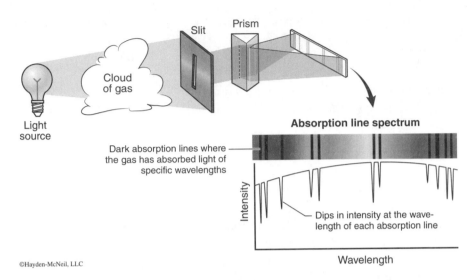

©Hayden-McNeil, LLC

Figure 8-6. Helium absorption spectrum.

Because **quantitative absorption spectroscopy** can be done at room temperature, it is the more common quantitative technique. It is usually performed on samples dissolved in solution. In clinical labs, determinations of the amounts of compounds like glucose and cholesterol in blood and urine samples employ this technique. By making absorbance measurements at various wavelengths and then plotting the results, one can create what is known as an **absorbance spectrum**. Figure 8-7 is an example of such a spectrum. Absorbance spectra are like fingerprints. Each compound has its own unique spectrum. In some cases this can be used to identify the presence of certain compounds in a sample. More often, it is used to determine the amount of compound present.

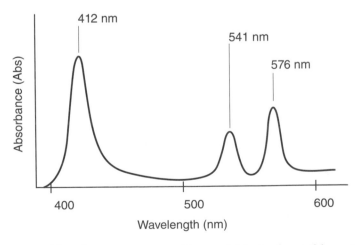

Figure 8-7. Absorbance spectrum of hemoglobin in the visible region.

8-3 SPECTROMETERS

A spectroscope is a device for separating light into its compontent wavelengths. A **spectrometer** is a spectroscope that has some sort of meter attached that can **measure** the *amount* of light (number of photons) at specific wavelengths. Thus, it is designed to provide a numerical measure of the amount of light emitted or absorbed at a particular wavelength. It is constructed so that the wavelength can be varied by the operator, and the amount of radiation absorbed or transmitted by the sample determined for each wavelength. In this way it is possible to learn which wavelengths of radiation are present and in what relative amounts.

Figure 8-8 is a schematic of a spectrometer. Light enters via the entrance slit and then passes through several parts: an objective lens, a grating, and an exit slit. This combination of parts functions as a **monochromator**, a device which selects only one color (actually, a narrow band of wavelengths) from all of the wavelengths/colors present in the source. A particular wavelength is selected, using the wavelength control, by adjusting the angle of the grating. This works because different wavelengths of light reflect off the grating at different angles. The net result is the separation of white light into a "rainbow" much like light transmitted through a prism of glass. The selected wavelength is at the center of the narrow band of wavelengths passing through the slit.

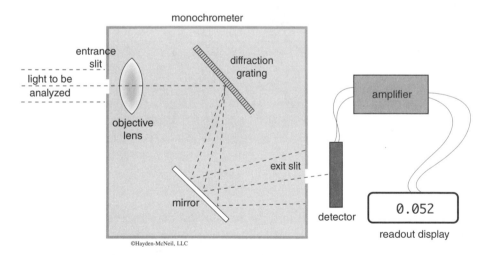

Figure 8-8. Schematic representation of a simple spectrometer.

The light then strikes a detector that generates a voltage in proportion to the intensity of the light hitting it. That voltage is then used to drive a read-out device that is designed to provide data in a useful way such as intensity.

As with all electronic devices, the design and operation of spectrometers has been greatly impacted by the developments of the latter half of the 20th century. Perhaps the most crucial was the development in the early '70s of the **Charged Coupled Device (CCD)**. Originally conceived as a new mode of data storage, it was soon discovered that CCDs held great promise as imaging devices. An imaging device is something that electronically mimics what photographic film does. Charged coupled devices consist of a number of elements between which charge can be shifted. In an image sensor, light falling on the array of elements produces a pattern of charges corresponding to the image. This image can then be electronically transported to some other location, such as a monitor, and reconstructed. CCDs were first employed to replace photographic plates in telescopes. The first such device was installed on the 1-meter telescope at Kitt Peak National Observatory in 1979. Today, CCDs are the detectors that make digital cameras not only possible, but affordable.

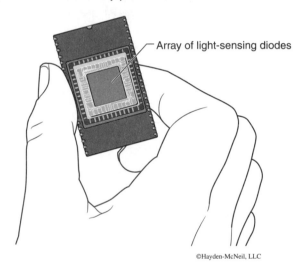

Array of light-sensing diodes

©Hayden-McNeil, LLC

Figure 8-9. A charged coupled device.

Modern spectrometers replace both the exit slit and detector with a CCD array. It is no longer necessary to measure light intensity one wavelength at a time. The number of wavelengths that can be monitored simultaneously is determined by the number of elements in the CCD array. Figure 8-10 is a schematic of a spectrometer outfitted with a CCD array. The array generates an output that can be used to reconstruct the intensity of light striking each of the elements in the array. This output can be sent to a monitor or printed directly. The output is instantaneous across the spectrum. No longer is it necessary to "scan" back and forth across the spectrum to identify light intensity at individual wavelengths.

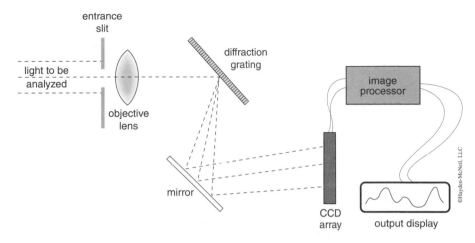

Figure 8-10. Schematic representation of a CCD spectrometer.

Spectrophotometers

Since spectrometers measure the amount of light entering the instrument, they are most often used for emission spectroscopy. In order to perform absorption spectroscopy, a light source of known intensity is required. An instrument that includes such a light source is known as a **spectrophotometer**. It is constructed so that the sample to be studied can be irradiated with light of known wavelength and intensity. The wavelength can be varied and the amount of radiation absorbed or transmitted by the sample determined for each wavelength. From this information, an absorption spectrum for a species can be obtained and used for both qualitative and quantitative determinations.

Spectrophotometers measure the amount of light transmitted by a sample and then convert this to more useful measures. One is the ratio of the transmitted light to the incident light, expressed as a percent. This is known as the **percent transmittance** (%T).

The %T calculation is easy to design into a spectrophotometer and was a common output before the advent of computer chips. A more useful quantity is the **absorbance, A or Abs**, because it is directly related to the concentration of the chemical species doing the absorbing.

There is an assumption inherent in the calculation of either %T or absorbance. The assumption is that all light not transmitted to the detector is absorbed by the chemical compounds in the solution. Two other possibilities exist. One is that the light is being scattered by the solution. Samples containing solid material, or which are cloudy, are difficult to analyze using a spectrophotometer. Samples encountered in the commercial world (biological fluids, soil solutions, etc.) are often cloudy and extra steps must be employed before analysis by absorption spectrophotometry can begin.

The other possibility is that light might be scattered or absorbed by the container used to hold the solution. Care must be taken to ensure that the **sample cells** do not affect the measurement. The cells (called *cuvets*) must be constructed of absolutely clear glass or plastic. If measurements are to be made below 350 nm, they must be made of quartz glass. Regular glasses are opaque below 350 nm.

THE SPECTRONIC 20

The best known and most widely used spectrophotometer ever built is the Spectronic 20®. You may have already used one in high school or in a biology class. First introduced in 1954, this rugged and reliable instrument provides accurate absorbance readings in the 400 to 650 nm range. What it does not do is provide complete spectra: it only provides single readings at single wavelengths. It is also not very reliable in the near ultraviolet range where many biological compounds absorb.

8-4 OCEAN OPTICS INSTRUMENTS

The spectrometers available for your use are small devices made by Ocean Optics that connect to computers and are operated by the Vernier Logger *Pro* program. Two different versions are available—the Red Tide (Figure 8-11) and the USB 4000 (Figure 8-12). They are operated identically. Both are contained in a small box connected to the computer via a USB port. These instruments generate spectra in the 200 to 900 nm range and can be used for both emission and absorption measurements.

Light is brought into the spectrometer using an optical cable. The light is converted into an electrical signal that is sent on to the computer. There the image processing software, **Logger Pro**, converts the signal into a display as illustrated in Figure 8-13. The general operation of Logger *Pro* is discussed in more detail in

Chapter 2. If a spectrometer is plugged into a USB port of the computer, Logger *Pro* will find it when the software is loaded. The default mode will be "absorbance." If emission measurements are required then the mode will need to be changed to "intensity."

Figure 8-11. Ocean Optics Red Tide Spectrometer.

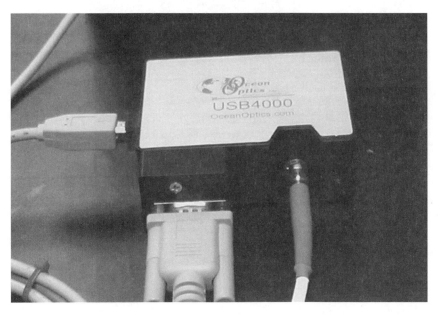

Figure 8-12. Ocean Optics USB 4000 Spectrometer.

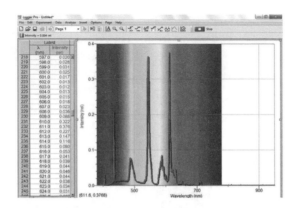

Figure 8-13. Fluorescent light spectrum.

8-5 PERFORMING EMISSION SPECTROSCOPY

To perform emission spectroscopy the light to be evaluated must be brought into the spectrometer. When using Ocean Optics spectrometers, this is done using an optical cable. Figure 8-14 shows an emission setup.

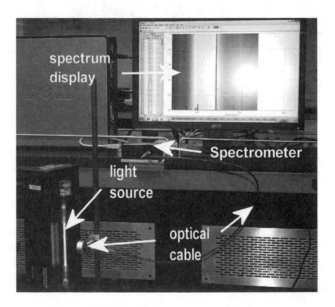

Figure 8-14. Emission spectroscopy setup.

The optical cable is aligned on the light source. It directs the light into the spectrometer, which generates a signal that is sent to the computer and processed by the Logger *Pro* program. The display shows a graph of the signal intensity at each of the measured wavelengths. The number of data points is so numerous the display appears to be a continuous spectrum. Figure 8-13 shows the emission spectrum of a fluorescent light.

To get Logger *Pro* to display an emission spectrum, the instrument must be put into the **intensity** mode. When in the intensity mode, the instrument essentially counts the number of photons striking the detector in a given period of time.

Figure 8-15 shows how to find the control that puts the spectrometer in intensity mode. Once selected, the spectrometer will display a graph of wavelength vs. intensity and the spreadsheet to the left of the graph will contain the raw data. Every wavelength the instrument measures will be listed along with the current intensity for that wavelength.

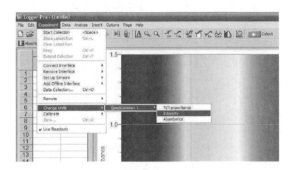

Figure 8-15. Selecting intensity mode.

Procedure for Making Emission Spectra and Measurements

1. Make sure the computer is running.

2. Make sure the spectrometer is connected to a USB port.

3. Start the software by selecting the Logger *Pro* icon.

4. Switch Logger *Pro* to the intensity mode as shown in Figure 8-15.

    Experiment > Change Units > Spectrometer 1 > Intensity.

Logger Pro
3.8.3

You are now ready to make emission measurements. Point the optical cable to your desired light source and select the green ▶Collect button from the toolbar. The instrument will now continuously read intensity and display it on-screen until the red ■Stop button is selected.

Procedure for Making Flame Emissions

Flame emission is a convenient way to heat atoms and ions to the point where they emit light and also suspend them in front of an optical cable so that the light can be collected. The sample is introduced into the base of a flame and carried up in the hot gases produced by the flame. The optical cable is aligned above the flame at a distance suitable for catching the light being emitted. Figure 8-16 illustrates such an arrangement.

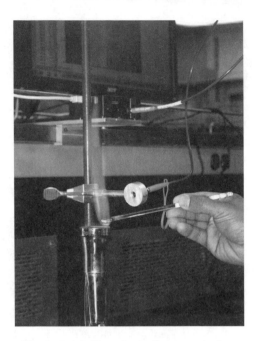

Figure 8-16. Creating a flame emission.

A flame is selected that does not produce its own light emissions in the wavelength range to be studied. For visible-range spectroscopy, a Meeker burner using natural gas (as pictured in Figure 8-16) is suitable.

Introducing the sample into the flame is the tricky part. Solid samples must be sufficiently finely divided to heat quickly and be carried up in the hot gases. Liquid samples must be concentrated enough to produce enough light to be seen. The ideal tool for holding samples is a quartz spatula, as shown in Figure 8-16. The biggest problem is that quartz, being a glass, breaks easily. While the spatula can handle the heat of the flame, it can't handle being dropped.

To use a quartz spatula to introduce sample:

1. Make sure the burner is not emitting any detectable light. If necessary, clean it. The burner can be cleaned with 1 M nitric acid, HNO_3. Put about a centimeter of the acid in a small beaker and dip the burner into the acid. Swirl for about a minute. Figure 8-17 illustrates this operation.

2. Clean the spatula by swirling in 1 M nitric acid, then heating until it no longer emits detectable light.

3. Put some of the sample onto the tip of the spatula.

4. Put the spatula into the base of the flame on the side of the flame closest to the optical cable (see Figure 8-16). Once the emission begins, hold in place until the signal is captured.

Figure 8-17. Cleaning the burner.

Nichrome spatulas or wires will also work, but have some issues. For solid salts, the salts tend to melt and drip onto the burner contaminating the surface of the burner. For liquids, due to the small volumes the spatula can carry, the emission duration is very short. If quartz spatulas are not available, you will use a nichrome spatula or wire.

8-6 PERFORMING ABSORPTION SPECTROSCOPY

The Ocean Optics spectrometers can make absorbance measurements when used with a calibrated light source. Three different light sources are available for your use. In each case the light source consists of a box containing the light and a cuvet holder. Two of the sources are connected to the spectrometer via an optical cable. For the third, the light source is bolted directly to the spectrometer.

The **visible spectrophotometer** will use one of two light sources. The tungsten light source is pictured in Figure 8-18. Its spectrum is shown in Figure 8-19. Notice that not much light is generated below 450 nm. This light source is not good for measuring absorbance at wavelengths in this part of the spectrum, a particularly important consideration since many biochemical measurements are made between 300 and 400 nm.

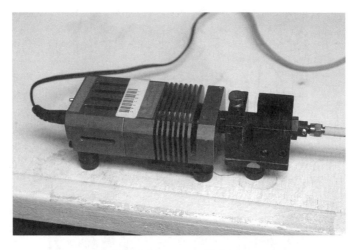

Figure 8-18. Tungsten light source.

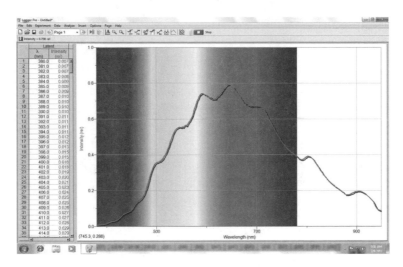

Figure 8-19. Tungsten lamp output.

The other visible light source used with the spectrometers is contained in a box bolted to the spectrometer (Figure 8-20). This has an output similar to the one shown in Figure 8-19. When using one of these, you need to be cognizant of the direction light passes through the cuvet holder.

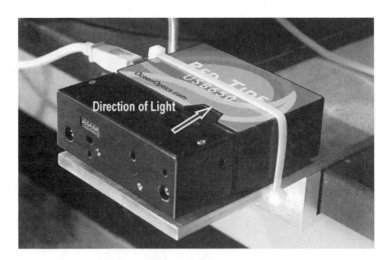

Figure 8-20. Visible light source.

The **ultraviolet (UV) spectrophotometer** uses a combination deuterium/tungsten light source pictured in Figure 8-21. Its spectrum is shown in Figure 8-22. The deuterium source adds significant light in the 200 to 400 nm range. This is the required light source for ultraviolet measurements.

Figure 8-21. UV light source.

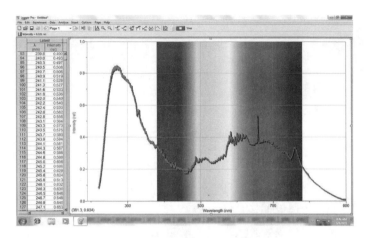

Figure 8-22. UV lamp output.

To measure absorbance, the spectrophotometer must be calibrated. This is done by first recording the number of counts at each of the 2048 elements from the pure light source as it passes through a reference solution. Next, the number of counts when the light source is blocked is recorded. Both of these operations are automatically performed by the software when the appropriate buttons are pushed.

Once the instrument has been calibrated and a sample is inserted into the holder, the computer calculates the ratio of the counts hitting the detector to the stored reference counts for each of the 2048 elements, converts these into absorbance values, and plots the result on the screen. Of course, the computer operates at a speed that makes all this appear to happen instantaneously.

Measuring Absorbance using Logger *Pro*

When turned on, the spectrometer will be in standby mode. The first thing you will need to do is to calibrate it. Do so by selecting the calibration tool: ***Experiment > Calibrate > Spectrometer 1***. Figure 8-16 illustrates this.

1. The software will prompt you to allow the lamp to warm up. If you know the light source is already warm you can skip the warm-up step.

2. Put a cuvet containing your blank solution in the sample holder when prompted.

3. Select "finish calibration" when prompted.

4. Select OK.

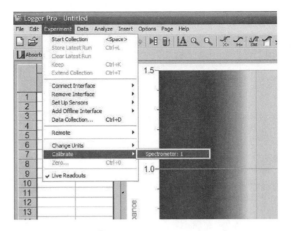

Figure 8-23. Calibrating the spectrometer.

You are now ready to make absorbance measurements. To start, select the ▶Collect button from the toolbar. The instrument will now continuously read absorbance and display it on-screen until the ∎Stop button is selected. The spectrum is displayed on the right. The actual wavelength and absorbance readings are given in the data columns on the left.

Notice that no further adjustments to the spectrometer can be made while in the data collection mode. To re-calibrate the spectrometer or make other changes you will need to first stop data collection.

To highlight a particular wavelength use the "examine" function. This allows you to select a point on the graph using the cursor. The corresponding data points will be highlighted in the table. This function is toggled on and off using either control+E or the ⚓ icon on the toolbar.

There are a number of different data collection configurations for using the spectrometers. Each such configuration is saved as a file that can be loaded from the File menu. By selecting "File > Open" you will be able to see the menu. When such a file is required you will be instructed to load up that file.

Figure 8-24. Logger *Pro* toolbar.

9

POTENTIOMETRIC MEASUREMENTS

Electric potential is something that can be easily measured and quantified. This makes it a useful tool in the lab. This chapter discusses the following.

+ pH electrodes.

+ Ion-selective electrodes.

Traditionally, measurements of chemical composition are tedious. The ideal measurement device would be a "probe" that could be pointed at or placed in the sample and would generate a "readout" of the various chemical properties. The Star Trek "tricorder" is an example of such a device. While the ideal is currently realized only in fiction, a number of such devices are currently available. Commonly referred to as "sensors," they vary greatly in terms of their cost, reliability, and suitability for particular kinds of analysis. New sensors are being developed all the time and are revolutionizing many industries by providing much more information faster and more precisely than previously possible. Perhaps the most well-known examples are in the practice of medicine, in which the information provided by sensors has made precise diagnosis more feasible and microsurgery more practical.

Figure 9-1. Tricorder.

9-1 ION-SELECTIVE ELECTRODES

Potentiometric measurements require measuring the potential difference between two electrochemical cells. One of the cells is designed to be dependent on the chemical of interest, while the other provides a constant, reference potential. The cells are contained in electrodes. Often, both cells are contained in the same electrode. The electrode, or electrodes, are placed in the sample of interest and the potential difference measured. Once the electrode(s) has been calibrated against standard solutions, the potential measurements can be converted directly into concentrations.

By far the most common potentiometric measuring device is the pH meter and pH electrode, but others are becoming more common. Glucometers are now replacing glucose test strips as the preferred means of measuring glucose levels in blood samples. These devices are now quite commonly used by patients to monitor glucose levels wherever they might be. And the advent of ever smaller electrodes has made it possible to use potentiometric techniques to measure concentrations within living cells.

A pH electrode is one specific example of a class of sensors known as ion-selective electrodes (ISEs). It is designed to be specific for hydronium ion (H_3O^+). An ion-selective electrode is placed into a sample solution and is connected to a potentiometer. If the conditions of the measurement are well understood and controlled, the measured potential can be related to the concentration of the specific chemical species the electrode was designed to measure.

A typical ISE is schematically represented in Figure 9-2. The most important part of the ISE is the "membrane" at the front of the electrode, which separates the internal filling solution from the solution to be characterized. This "membrane" can take several forms; it can be a polymer, embedded with any number of sensing agents, it can be a tailored composition glass membrane, or a thin sheet of an insoluble salt, such as $AgBr$, LaF_3, etc. Each ISE has a specific ion for which it is used in analytical situations, and the composition of this "membrane" is different for each ion to be detected.

The pH electrode uses a special glass membrane that allows the electrode to selectively follow changes in solution H_3O^+ concentration. A commercial analytical laboratory may possess more than 10 different ISEs, each targeted to a specific ion!

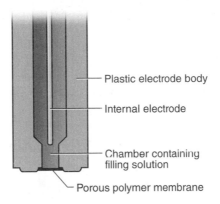

- Plastic electrode body
- Internal electrode
- Chamber containing filling solution
- Porous polymer membrane

Figure 9-2. Schematic of an ion-selective electrode.

The function of the potentiometer (volt meter) is to measure the potential between the two electrochemical cells. This potential is expressed across the selective "membrane" and varies with the changing concentration of the selected ion in solution. The pH meter, when used with a pH electrode, is typically calibrated so that changes in potential across the glass membrane are automatically converted to changes in pH. When using an ISE, the potential changes are used to create a calibration plot that can then be used to make the conversion from potential to ion concentration.

The potentiometer actually senses the *difference in potential* between the internal electrode of the ISE (in contact with a filling solution containing a known and fixed concentration of the ion to be measured), and another reference electrode in the solution to be analyzed, which contains the ion whose concentration you want to measure (Figure 9-3). Some ISEs, and the pH electrode, incorporate this external reference electrode into the body of the ISE, so that it appears that there may be only one electrode attached to the wires connected to the potentiometer. Both configurations, however, measure the changes that occur in interfacial potential across the membrane in response to changes in the concentration of the ion to be detected.

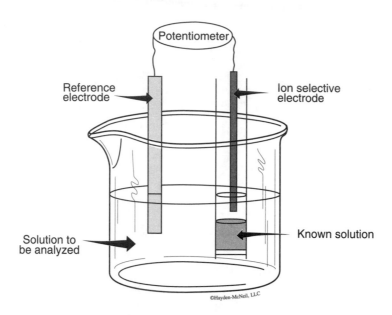

Figure 9-3. Schematic of potentiometer connected to
an ISE and a reference electrode.

The potential measured by the potentiometer at 25°C can be expressed as follows:

$$E_{cell} = C + (0.0591/z) \log [\text{ion}] \qquad (9\text{-}1)$$

where z represents the charge on the ion being analyzed, and contains the sign of
that ion ($z_K^+ = +1$; $z_{NO_3^-} = -1$; $z_{Ca+2} = +2$).

Equation 9-1 suggests that a plot of cell potential (E_{cell}) versus the log of the ion
concentration will be linear, with a slope (at 25°C) of 0.0591/z volts per decade
change in concentration of the ion, as illustrated in Figure 9-4.

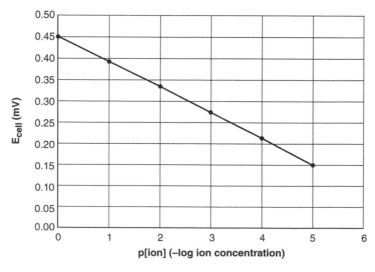

Figure 9-4. Plot of potentiometer response versus solution concentration.

NOTE

The value of the constant, C, will vary from system to system. The shape of the plot shown in Figure 9-4 is representative of what to expect in the lab, but the actual E_{cell} values may well be different.

Meters

Traditionally, the volt meters used to make potentiometric measurements have been stand-alone devices. The most common meter is a pH meter that also has a millivolt function. But computers are well suited for making potentiometric measurements, and the traditional meters are being replaced with computer-based software. In this course, you may be asked to use either a meter or the Vernier Logger *Pro* software to process the data provided by ion selective electrodes.

There are a wide variety of meters available for making pH measurements. They come with many different controls and the terminology will vary from one instrument to another. Here are the critical ones.

Power. Most, but not all, instruments have a power switch. Those that don't are on all the time once they are plugged in.

Function. Since pH meters are really potential meters, they usually have some control for switching between pH measurement mode and potential (millivolt) mode.

Standby. Some instruments have a switch for turning the electrode on and off. It is often called the "standby" or "read" switch. If your meter has one, make sure it remains in the *standby mode* unless a measurement is actually being made. Some meters have an indicator light that lights up when it is actively measuring. It should be off unless in use.

Calibration. Most meters will have one or more controls used to calibrate the meter and electrode. For a two-point calibration (described below) two adjustments are required. These are most often designated the "slope" and "intercept" controls.

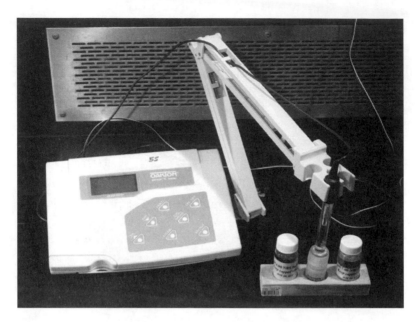

Figure 9-5. pH meter and electrode.

9-2 pH ELECTRODES

These come in many different styles. They all consist of two electrochemical cells encased in a glass or plastic body. At one end is the glass bulb. This is the part that "senses" the pH. It is very fragile and should be treated like fine crystal glass. Many electrodes come equipped with an epoxy resin body that extends below the glass bulb to help prevent accidental breakage. The electrode measures the potential at the surface of the glass bulb. For this to work properly the bulb must be completely immersed in the solution being measured. Some electrodes come with a storage cap. This must be removed before using or the bulb will not contact the solution to be measured.

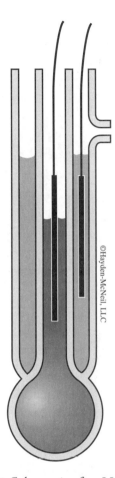

Figure 9-6. Schematic of a pH electrode.

In a stagnant solution, the pH at the surface of the bulb will change. After some time the measured potential will no longer match the potential in the rest of the solution. To prevent this, the solution must be constantly stirred. This can be done by hand, but a magnetic stirrer is better.

Vibration will also cause the electrode to give false or inaccurate readings. The stirring must be arranged in such a fashion that the bulb is not being jostled by the stir bar or stir rod.

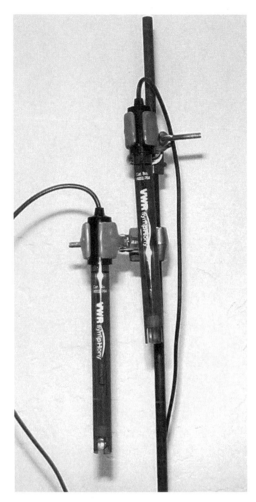

Figure 9-7. pH electrodes.

Two-Point Calibration of a pH Electrode and a Stand-Alone Meter

pH meters contain circuitry that allows the meter to be calibrated to read pH values directly from the meter. Calibration is accomplished by placing the electrode in an appropriate buffer solution and adjusting the circuits. The "intercept" circuit is adjusted with the electrode in a pH 7 solution. The "slope" circuit is adjusted with the electrode in a pH 4 or a pH 10 solution. The choice of the pH for the slope circuit adjustment is based on the anticipated pH values to be measured. For acidic measurements, a pH 4 solution is preferred. For basic measurements, pH 10 is preferred.

Once these circuits have been set, the meter can be used to measure pH. If the knobs are moved, however, or if the meter is moved, or if the electrode connection is changed in any way, the meter will have to be recalibrated.

1. Obtain the required two buffered standards. Don't forget to clean and rinse all glassware used to avoid contamination and dilution errors. One standard should have a pH value of **7.00**. The other should be either **4.00** or **10.00**.

2. Make sure you have a squeeze bottle with distilled water handy and select a beaker to use to catch rinse water.

3. Every time the electrode is moved from one solution to another, thoroughly rinse the glass tip with distilled water and blot it dry with a Kimwipe.

4. Place the electrode in the pH 7 buffer solution and make sure the glass bulb is fully immersed. Stir the buffer for about 30 seconds. If using a stir plate, make sure the stir bar is not striking the electrode. If the meter has a standby mode, switch it to "read." Adjust the intercept control until the meter displays "7.00." Return the meter to "standby" mode.

5. Remove the electrode from the pH 7 buffer, rinse it with distilled water and put it into the other pH buffer solution. Stir the buffer for thirty seconds. With the meter in "read" mode, adjust the slope control until the meter displays the pH value of the buffer being used. Return the meter to "standby" mode.

6. Repeat steps 4 and 5 as many times as is necessary until no further adjustment of the slope and intercept controls are required. When this occurs, place the electrode in a beaker of distilled water for temporary storage. It is normal to have to repeat this procedure up to five times. If after five repetitions you feel the readings have not begun to stabilize, consult your instructor.

7. You are now ready to measure pH values. Put the electrode in the solution you wish to measure. Stir the solution and put the meter in "read" mode. Read the pH value. Return the meter to "standby" mode.

Two-Point Calibration of a pH Electrode for Vernier Logger *Pro*

Calibration is accomplished by placing the electrode in an appropriate buffer solution and adjusting the software to read the correct value. For most applications two such buffers are required. One should be a pH 7.00 solution. The second should be either pH 4.00 or pH 10.00. The choice of pH for the second solution is based on the anticipated pH values to be measured. For acidic measurements, a pH 4.00 solution is preferred. For basic measurements, pH 10.00 is preferred.

Setting Up the pH Probe and Interface

1. Obtain an **Electrode Amplifier** with **Go!Link** interface attached. (Figure 9-8).

2. Carefully connect a pH probe to the **Electrode Amplifier** BNC jack—*Do not force, the connection is fragile!*

3. Connect the **Go!Link** interface to a computer USB port.

4. Note that multiple pH probes can be simultaneously connected to one computer. The limit is the number of USB ports on the computer.

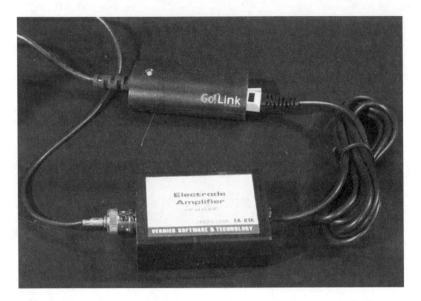

Figure 9-8. Vernier Electrode Amplifier with Go!Link interface.

Calibration

1. Obtain the required two buffered standards: 7.00 and either 4.00 or 10.00 (see discussion above).

2. Make sure you have a squeeze bottle with distilled water handy and select a beaker to use to catch rinse water.

3. Every time the electrode is moved from one solution to another, thoroughly rinse the glass tip with distilled water and blot it dry.

4. Start the **Logger Pro** software. Logger Pro 3.8.3

5. Select **Experiments/Calibration/GoLink: X/Electrode Amplifier**, where "X" is the number the software assigned to the pH probe.

6. The **Calibration** dialogue box will open (Figure 9-9). On the right, under **Current Calibration,** make sure it says **Electrode Amp pH <Computer>**. If not, click on the drop-down menu and select it.

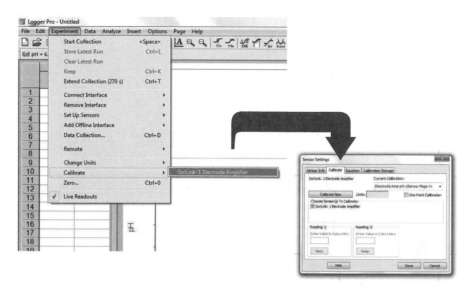

Figure 9-9. Calibrating a pH electrode.

7. Next click **Calibrate Now.**

8. Remove the pH probe from the storage solution. Rinse with DI water. Gently dry the tip with a Kimwipe. Place in the 4.00 pH (or 10.00 pH) buffer.

9. Let probe equilibrate for 20–30 seconds.

10. Next, in the **Reading 1**: sub-window, enter 4.00 (or 10.00) in **Enter Value in Data Units** box. Click **Keep.**

11. **Reading 2**: sub-window will activate.

12. Remove the pH probe from the 4.00 (or 10.00) buffer. Rinse with DI water. Gently wipe tip with Kimwipe. Place in the 7.00 pH buffer.

13. Let probe equilibrate for 20–30 seconds.

14. In the **Reading 2**: sub-window, enter 7.00 in **Enter Value in Data Units box.** Click **Keep.**

15. Click **Done.**

9-3 OTHER ION-SELECTIVE ELECTRODES

A pH electrode is far and away the most common ion-selective electrode (ISE) you are likely to encounter in a lab. But it is not the only one. There are a great variety of electrodes designed to measure the concentrations of many common ions. Presented here is a general procedure for measuring solution concentrations using an ion-selective electrode. Before doing so, make sure you are familiar with any special procedures or conditions that might be required, particularly those involving storage of the electrode.

1. Electrode Setup

Identify the electrode setup that you will use. Read any instructions provided in lab for its use. Inspect the meter and electrodes. Describe in your notebook (a drawing would be better) the way the electrodes are stored. Make sure you record sufficient details to ensure you can leave the electrode(s) and meter the way you find them. If you encounter problems, see your instructor.

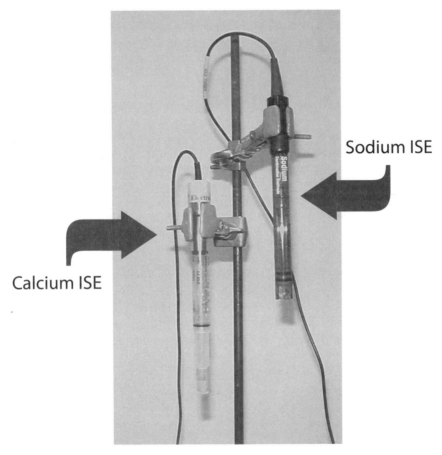

Figure 9-10. Ion-selective electrodes.

©Hayden-McNeil, LLC

Figure 9-11. Electrode tip.

CAUTION

For an electrode like the one in Figure 9-11, the tip is a thin polymer membrane formed on the end of a short piece of tygon tubing. It is fragile. Please handle it carefully. *Do not* remove the tygon tip from the electrode. Do not touch the membrane or allow it to come in contact with anything, especially a stir bar.

2. Ionic Strength Adjustor

Potentiometric measurements depend on the conductivity of the solution being measured. To obtain reliable measurements, the conductivity of all solutions being measured should be the same. This is achieved by using an **ionic strength adjustor:** a solution that is added to every sample. The solution best suited to use as an ionic strength adjustor will be different for each kind of electrode. Table 9-1 lists some recommended solutions. Two mL per 100 mL of sample is the recommended amount to use.

Table 9-1. Recommended ionic strength adjustor solutions.

Ion	ISA
sodium	4 M in NH_4Cl and 4 M in NH_4OH
calcium	4 M KCl
chloride	5 M $NaNO_3$
nitrate	2 M $(NH_4)_2SO_4$
lead	5 M $NaClO_4$
copper	5 M $NaNO_3$

3. Making Standard Solutions

Calibration of an ion-selective electrode requires a series of solutions containing the specific ion in known concentrations. Pure, solid samples of known molecular weight are the best source. The easiest way to make a series of solutions of known concentrations is to prepare a stock solution and then perform a serial dilution (Chapter 11). When deciding what solutions to make, keep the following in mind.

+   The concentrations of your standard solutions should bracket the manufacturer's stated range for the electrode. Because you will need to convert your concentrations into logs, it is best if the standard solutions have concentrations of the form 1.00×10^x M, where x will vary from 0 to –7.

+   Determining the linearity of the calibration plot is crucial for proper evaluation of its reliability. A minimum of four standard solutions should be employed.

+   To compensate for ionic strength effects, an ionic strength adjustor solution should be added to every solution including the standards. Two mL per 100 mL of sample is recommended.

4. Measuring Potentials of Standards and Checking for Proper Electrode Function

When all solutions are ready and the electrode is properly prepared, potential measurement can begin. Measure the potential of all your standard solutions, one at a time, beginning with the least concentrated solution. You always want to begin measurement with the least concentrated as the act of potential measurement desensitizes the electrode to a small extent.

Some issues you will need to face while making these measurements are:

+   Stirring of samples to be measured. To obtain a constant potential reading, the solution must be stirred. Stir plates and stir bars are recommended. Constant, reliable readings require that the stir bar does not contact the electrode and the vortex does not expose the electrode to air.

+ Dilution errors continue to be a concern. All glassware and stir bars must be either dry or rinsed with the solution to be measured. The electrode is normally blotted dry rather than being rinsed.

+ The appropriate beaker size should be given some forethought. It needs to be big enough to accommodate the electrodes and the stir bar, but small enough that the solution depth will cover the electrode.

+ Once you begin the calibration process you must be careful to avoid disturbing the system. Even seemingly minor disturbances could invalidate your calibration. You must not adjust any of the settings on the pH meter. In addition you should try to avoid moving the wires any more than is necessary. It is recommended that you move the electrodes only by the holder to avoid altering their potentials.

Once you have measured the potential of your most concentrated standard solution, place the electrode in a beaker of distilled water to soak. This is to counter the desensitization mentioned above.

Plot your potentials against the log of the solution concentrations. Determine if the slope is linear through the pertinent part of the plot. If it is not, or if you're not sure, consult your instructor before continuing.

5. Measuring Potential of Samples

Once the electrode is calibrated it can be used to measure appropriate sample solutions. All of the issues mentioned above for the calibration measurements also apply to the sample measurements. Appropriate samples are those that do not interact with the electrode. Particularly concentrated solutions are bad because they will significantly desensitize the electrode. Milk, paint, and other such solutions are not good because they will coat the electrode with a film that will prevent measurement and ruin the electrode!

When you have finished all measurements, turn off the meter. Dispose of all solutions in the appropriate waste bottle. Return all borrowed equipment to the prep-room.

6. Measuring Potential Using Logger Pro

Check the ISE and Interface Setup

1. Confirm that the ISE is connected to the **Electrode Amplifier** BNC jack— *Do not force, connection is fragile!*

2. Confirm **Electrode Amplifier** is attached to the **Go!Link** interface

3. Confirm the **Go!Link** interface is connected to a computer USB port

4. Note: Up to four ISEs can be run from a single computer.

Calibration and Sample Readings

5. Start the **Logger Pro** software.   Logger Pro
                                              3.8.3

6. Check the reading in the lower left of the screen. If it is reading mV, continue on to step 9. If not, you will have to change the data collection mode.

7. Select the **GO** icon on the left side of the navigation bar (see Figure 9-12).

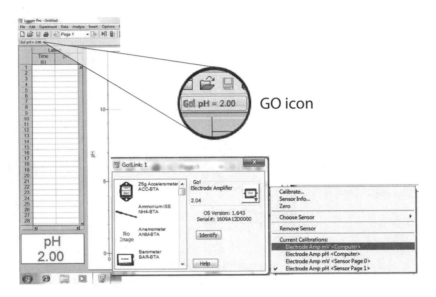

Figure 9-12. Configuring Logger *Pro* for potential measurements.

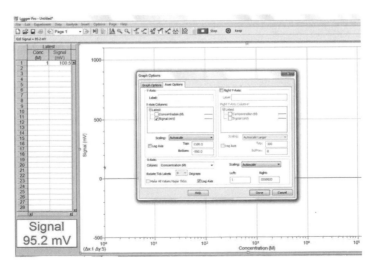

Figure 9-13. Configuring graph to properly diplay ISE measurements.

8. The **GoLink:***X* dialogue box will open. On the right, in the "Electrode Amplifier" box, click on the electrode amplifier icon. Under **Current Calibration** select **Electrode Amp mV <Computer>.**

9. Remove ISE from the storage solution. Rinse with the appropriate rinse solution (*never* tap water!). For calcium ISE use the lab distilled water. For a sodium ISE use the designated sodium ISE rinse solution. *Very gently* (electrode membrane is very easily damaged) dab tip with Kimwipe. Place in lowest concentration calibration solution.

10. Let probe equilibrate for 30 seconds. Probe end must be submerged in at least 2 cm of solution to read accurately.

11. Click ▶Collect.

12. Now click ■Stop to end data collection.

13. Move probe to the next-most dilute calibration. Let probe equilibrate for 20–30 seconds.

14. Click ▶Collect When the "Save" dialogue box opens, choose **Store Latest Run** to store the previous data (*do not* select "Erase and Continue," or you will have to start over).

15. Repeat 8 and 9 for the remaining calibration solutions, then *immediately* follow with your unknown

Return ISE probe to its proper storage condition. For probes stored in a solution, do not allow it to dry out!

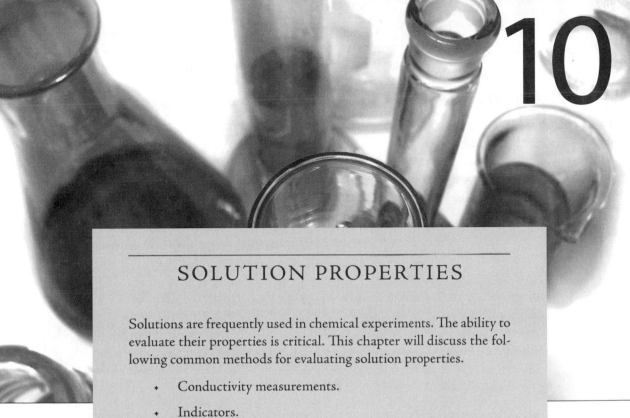

SOLUTION PROPERTIES

Solutions are frequently used in chemical experiments. The ability to evaluate their properties is critical. This chapter will discuss the following common methods for evaluating solution properties.

- Conductivity measurements.
- Indicators.
- Acid–base titrations.
- Complexometric titrations.
- Spectrophotometric quantification.

Solutions have a number of properties that can be evaluated and there are a variety of techniques for doing so. Mass, volume, and temperature are pretty straightforward. Phase changes are discussed in Chapter 7. The evaluation of the interaction of solutions with light is known as spectroscopy and is discussed in Chapter 8. The major value of spectroscopy is measuring the composition of solutions, a particularly common analysis. Chapter 9 describes potentiometric measurements, which can provide rather precise concentration measurements. This chapter will present a number of other techniques for analyzing the composition of solutions that make use of measuring devices described in previous chapters.

The evaluation of solution composition can involve both qualitative and quantitative analysis. **Qualitative analysis** is concerned with the identification of the various things present in the solution. It answers the question "what is it?" **Quantitative analysis** is the determination of the amounts of things present in solutions. It answers the question "how much is there?" Due to the nature of solutions, quantitative analyses usually provide answers in terms of **concentration**— amounts per unit volume.

10-1 CONDUCTIVITY MEASUREMENTS

Although pure water does not conduct electricity, solutions do. The degree to which a solution conducts is a property that can provide useful information about that solution. Such measurements are routinely employed in industry and research to monitor water and its purity.

Conductivity is the ability of a material or a solution to conduct an electrical current. In science, it is defined as the inverse of resistance. It is obtained by measuring the resistance between two electrodes placed in the solution. The conductivity is given by

$$C = \frac{d}{RA}$$

(10-1)

where R is the resistance, A the area of the electrodes, and the d the distance between them. It is measured in units of **Siemens.** One Siemen (also known as the mho) is equal to one ampere per volt or 1/ohms.

You will have available for your use a Vernier conductivity sensor designed to be used with Logger *Pro*. It consists of a tubular probe attached to a control box which is in turn connected to a GoLink (Figure 10-1). The probe contains two electrodes in a housing open to the solution, but designed to protect the electrodes from contact with things that might disturb the reading. It is constructed so that d and A in Equation 10-1 will remain constant. The sensor is calibrated at the time of manufacture and does not need to be calibrated by the user. When operating the sensor, Logger *Pro* will display the conductivity in units of microsiemens, μS.

Figure 10-1. Conductivity sensor.

Using the Conductivity Sensor

1. Start the **Logger *Pro*** software.

   Logger Pro
   3.8.3

2. Rinse the tip of the conductivity probe with distilled water.

3. Insert the tip of the probe into the sample to be tested. Be sure the electrode surfaces in the elongated cell are completely submerged in the liquid.

4. While gently swirling the probe, wait for the display reading to stabilize. This should take no more than 5 to 10 seconds.

5. Rinse the end of the probe with distilled water before taking another measurement.

6. When you have finished using the conductivity probe, thoroughly rinse it with distilled water making sure to rinse the cavity where the electrodes are. Blot the probe dry using a paper towel or Kimwipe. The probe is stored dry.

CAUTIONS

1. If you are concerned about water droplets diluting or contaminating the sample to be tested, blot the inside of the electrode cell dry with a Kimwipe.
2. If you are taking readings at temperatures below 15°C or above 30°C, allow more time for the temperature compensation to adjust and provide a stable conductivity reading.
3. Do not place the electrode in viscous, organic liquids, such as heavy oils, glycerin (glycerol), or ethylene glycol. Do not place the probe in acetone or non-polar solvents, such as pentane or hexane.
4. Do not completely submerge the sensor. The handle is not waterproof.

10-2 INDICATORS

As the name implies, indicators are substances that indicate something. They can indicate the presence of things (qualitative analysis), they can indicate the amounts of things (quantitative analysis), or they can indicate both. They work by producing some kind of change that can be easily observed. Most indicators work by changing color, although those that form gases or precipitates are also known. The first indicator to be widely used was **litmus**: a large, complex biochemical assembly. A solution with a pH less than 5 will cause litmus to be red. A solution with a pH of more than 8 will cause litmus to be blue. Litmus is used to determine if a solution is acidic or basic. If the litmus turns red, the solution is acidic; if the solution turns blue, it is basic.

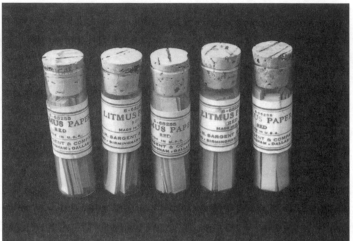

Figure 10-2. Litmus paper.

Indicators are often made up as concentrated solutions that are then added to the sample. One or two drops of the indicator solution are sufficient to impart color. Such indicators are often used to tell when a reaction is finished or a particular condition has been achieved. For other uses, the chemical indicator is absorbed onto a support. Most often the support is paper. The chemicals react with the compound of interest to produce a colored product in which the color is proportional to the concentration. Some common examples are pool test kits, soil test kits, and pregnancy test strips. Clinical labs can test urine for more than 100 different molecules using urine test strips, but in the chemistry lab, the most common indicator strips measure pH.

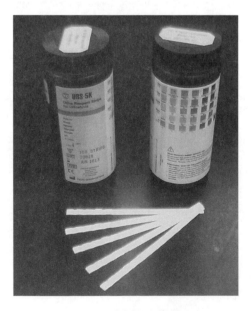

Figure 10-3. Urine test stips.

pH Indicator Paper

One of the more important properties of water is its acid/base chemistry. The degree of acidity or basicity of a water solution is expressed as the **pH**. Normally, the pH value will be somewhere between 0 and 14, although larger and smaller values are possible. Neutral solutions have a pH of 7. Acidic solutions have a pH less than 7. Basic solutions have a pH greater than 7.

The pH can dramatically affect many of the reactions that occur in water solutions. Measurement of pH is thus an important and frequently employed technique. There are two common ways pH is measured. The use of indicators is the oldest, quickest, and cheapest technique. The use of a pH meter and electrode provides much greater accuracy, but is more time-consuming and expensive. When rough measurements are all that is needed, indicators are preferred.

A pH indicator is a molecule that exhibits different colors at different pH values. When an indicator is added to a water solution, the resulting color will "indicate" the pH. Most indicators exhibit two colors that change over a **pH range** of 1 to 2 (note: there are no units to pH). At pH values below that range, the indicator will exhibit one color. At pH values above that range, the other color will be apparent. In between, the color will be intermediate between the two extremes. The pH range over which the color changes is known as the "change range." When a solution produces a color in the change range, the indicator color can be "read" to produce a pH value. If the color is one of the extremes, the only conclusion that can be drawn is that the pH is either greater than or less than the change range.

Indicator paper is absorbant paper saturated with the indicator. The paper is wet with solution of interest and the resulting color compared to a chart (Figure 10-4).

Figure 10-4. Single indicator pH reference chart.

pH indicator paper is sold for many different ranges. It is also made using "universal indicator." This is a mixture of indicators selected to produce a smooth color change over the entire pH range, from red for very acidic solutions to blue for very basic solutions. Indicator paper made with universal indicator is commonly referred to simply as "pH paper" (Figure 10-5). pH paper can be read to the nearest 1 pH unit. Individual indicator papers can be read to the nearest 0.1 pH unit.

Figure 10-5. Universal pH indicator reference chart.

Using Indicator Paper

There are a few issues that need to be considered when using indicator paper.

1. **Wetting the paper.** Sticking the indicator paper into the solution to be tested is not recommended. Some of the indicator chemical would dissolve into the solution, thereby contaminating it. The preferred technique is to use a clean glass rod or micropipet. Wet the glass rod with the solution to be tested and touch it to the paper. The paper can then be compared to the reference chart to determine the pH. This approach also has the advantage of allowing the piece of paper to be used multiple times.

2. **Reading the paper.** The color comparison to the chart should be done quickly, particularly with solutions with pH values far from 7. The solution on the paper will almost immediately begin to react with acids and bases in the air, thereby changing the pH. Once dry, the color of the paper will no longer reflect the pH of the solution.

10-3 TITRATIONS

Titration is a general technique for determining the amount of a chemical substance present in a sample. First developed at the time of the American Revolution, titration is still a common technique in chemical laboratories because it is quick and easy to perform and doesn't require a lot of complicated (and expensive) equipment. A titration can be created in any situation governed by a chemical reaction of known stoichiometry, as long as there is a quick and reliable method for determining when the reaction is done.

A titration is performed by reacting the substance in question with a known amount of another substance until the unknown substance has been completely reacted. From the **stoichiometry** of the equation and the amount of known substance added, the amount of the unknown substance can be calculated. A titration can be performed based on any chemical reaction, if the following criteria are met.

1. The reaction between the known and the unknown substances must be of known stoichiometry. The most common kind of reaction is acid–base. But titrations based on complex ion formation and precipitation are also common.

2. The reaction must quickly proceed to completion. This is best achieved by reacting two solutions. One solution is added to the other with constant mixing to ensure quick and complete reaction.

3. There must be some method of determining when a stoichiometric equality has been achieved. This condition is referred to as the **endpoint** of the titration. Most often the endpoint is detected using an **indicator**. A suitable indicator will change color at the endpoint.

Titrations require two special glassware items, both designed for titrations. The **buret** allows the user to measure how much of a solution has been added when it is unknown at the start how much solution is required. The **Erlenmeyer flask** allows mixing by swirling without losing any of the contents. Both are discussed in Chapter four.

Titrations also require a **titrant**. This is the solution that will be reacted with the sample. It needs to be of known composition. The concentration of the titrant is known either because it was made very accurately from a known sample or it was **standardized** against a **primary standard**. The concentration of the titrant needs to be selected to produce a reasonable titration volume. Depending on the size of the buret available the target volume should be between 10 and 50 mL.

To perform a titration the buret and Erlenmeyer flask are arranged as shown in Figure 10-6. The sample is placed in the flask and the titrant in the buret. An appropriate indicator is added to the flask. If a magnetic stir plate is available a teflon-coated stir bar is added and a moderate rate of stirring established. Titrant is added from the buret until the indicator changes color. The rate of addition of the titrant is critical. If it is too fast the endpoint will be missed. This is referred to as over-shooting the endpoint. The preferred technique is to add titrant rather rapidly at first and then to slow down as the endpoint is approached. You will know when to slow down by watching for the color change. As you approach the endpoint, the place in the solution where the titrant lands will begin to change color then change back as it mixes in with the rest of the solution. This is the time to slow down.

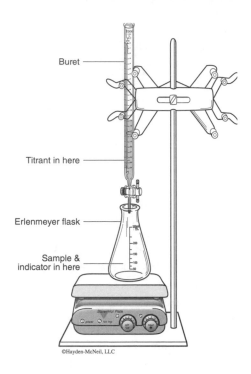

Buret

Titrant in here

Erlenmeyer flask

Sample &
indicator in here

©Hayden-McNeil, LLC

Figure 10-6. Titration setup.

10-4 ACID–BASE TITRATIONS

By far the most common titration is an **acid–base titration**. Acids and bases react to form water. When equal amounts of an acid and a base react, the resulting solution is said to be neutral. The governing equation is

$$H_3O^+ + OH^- \rightarrow 2\,H_2O \qquad (10\text{-}2)$$

The endpoint of an acid–base titration occurs when the sample solution has reached neutrality. At neutrality (pH 7),

$$\text{moles } H_3O^+ = \text{moles } OH^- \qquad (10\text{-}3)$$

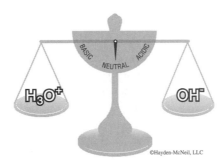

©Hayden-McNeil, LLC

Figure 10-7. Balancing the chemical reactants.

Titration is about balance—the balance between two components of a chemical reaction. The trick is determining when balance has been achieved. A successful titration is designed in such a way that it is easy to identify when balance has been achieved. Figure 10-7 graphically illustrates this balance for an acid–base titration.

In an acid–base titration, either the acid or the base can be the unknown quantity. You can start with either and add the other until neutrality is achieved. Consider starting with an acid in a flask and adding a base solution. Neutrality will be achieved when the moles of added base equal the moles of acid originally present in the reaction flask. The endpoint will be determined using an acid–base indicator. Two such indicators are commonly used. One is bromothymol blue (abbreviated BTB). Solutions containing this organic dye are yellow when the pH is less than 7 and blue when the pH is greater than 7. By looking for the appearance or disappearance of a green color in the solution, you will be able to tell when neutrality (pH 7) has been achieved. The other is **phenolphthalein**. This organic dye is pink when the pH is greater than 7 and colorless at values less than 7. By looking for the appearance or disappearance of the pink color you will be able to tell when the pH of a solution becomes 7.

Standardization of a Sodium Hyrdroxide Solution

As an example of an acid–base titration consider the standardization of a sodium hydroxide solution. The process of determining the concentration of an unknown solution is known as **standardization**. You will standardize a solution of NaOH by using a **primary standard**. This is a material having an exactly known composition and for which accurate weights or volumes can be measured. The primary standard is used to "standardize" unknown solutions.

Most acids cannot be used as primary standards because they soak up unknown amounts of water from the atmosphere and, as a result, do not have an exactly known composition. A suitable solid acid to use as a primary standard is **potassium hydrogen phthalate** (abbreviated KHP). From the weight of the KHP sample, and its molecular weight (204.22 g/mole), the **moles** of KHP can be calculated and equated to the **moles** of NaOH in the titration volume. Knowing the moles of NaOH and the volume (as measured by the buret) one can calculate the molarity (M).

Described here is one titration of a KHP primary standard with a sodium hydroxide solution having a concentration somewhere near to 0.1 M. The amount of primary standard has been selected to produce a titration volume of about 20 mL.

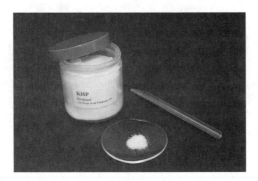

Figure 10-8. A watch glass containing about 1.2 g of KHP.

1. **Mass a sample of the primary standard**. Use potassium hydrogen phthalate (abbreviated KHP). The ideal sample size is about 0.5 g. The KHP can be massed directly in the Erlenmeyer flask or on weighing paper. If the latter, care must be taken to ensure the entire sample is transferred into the flask. The mass must be determined as accurately as possible.

2. **Dissolve the KHP**. Add about 50 mL of water. Swirl gently to dissolve the acid. This is a slow process. Swirl the flasks for several seconds every minute or two until solution is complete. Add 2–3 drops of indicator solution.

3. **Preparing to titrate**. Fill the buret with the NaOH solution to be standardized. Use a wash bottle to wash excess NaOH hanging from the buret tip. Read and record the solution level in the buret. Place a piece of white paper under the flask. This will help you see what is happening in the titration flask.

4. **Titrating**. The following is described for a titration using BTB as the indicator. With phenolphthalein the color change will be from colorless to pink. Place the flask holding your sample underneath the buret tip. Begin adding the NaOH. Swirl the flask and watch the color. At some point a green to blue color will begin to appear. Slow down the addition and continue to swirl. When the color is completely green to blue, stop adding the NaOH. Continue swirling. The color should fade back to yellow. Add more NaOH until the

color returns to green or blue. Again, swirl and watch to see if it fades back to yellow. Continue this process until the color remains green to blue for at least 30 seconds. This is the endpoint of the titration.

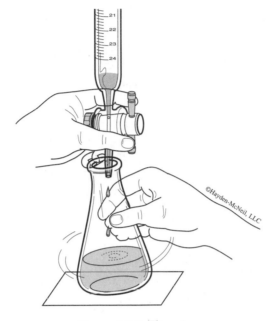

Figure 10-9. Titrating.

TECHNIQUE NOTES

1. If you use a funnel to fill the buret, make sure you re-move it before making any measurements. Solution dripping from the funnel would invalidate your mea-surements.
2. While adding titrant from the buret, some of this solu-tion will splash up on the inside walls of the flask. If left there, this will be solution that was measured, but not reacted. Swirling helps avoid error by mixing this solution in. It is also a good idea, when near the endpoint, to wash the inside walls of the container with a small stream of distilled water to ensure complete reaction.

5. **Repeat the Titration.** Repeat the titration as many times as possible to dem-onstrate reproducibility. Three titrations that agree within 1% is an absolute minimum. Four is better, and five better still. Since the weight of KHP is different for each trial, the volume of NaOH used will also vary. The ratio of the two, however, should not vary. For your results to be considered good, this ratio should not vary by more than 1% over the range of titrations.

10-5 WEAK ACID TITRATIONS

Simple titrations, as described previously, provide only one data point. By making many more measurements during the course of the titration, we can learn even more about the solution. Weak acid titrations use a pH electrode to measure the hydronium ion concentration of the solution over the course of the titration. They are primarily used to determine **weak acid dissociation constants, K_a**. The dissociation constant is an intensive property of the acid and can be used to identify a pure sample of the acid. The titration is based on the equilibrium involving water and weak acids.

$$HA + H_2O \rightleftharpoons H_3O^+ + A^- \tag{10-4}$$

The relative concentrations of the components of this equilibrium are described by the **weak acid dissociation constant, K_a**

$$K_a = \frac{[H_2O^+]_{eq}[A^-]_{eq}}{[HA]_{eq}} \tag{10-5}$$

where $[X]_{eq}$ is the equilibrium concentration of component X in moles/L. K_a is a constant for a given acid at a given temperature. Determining the K_a of a weak acid requires establishing an equilibrium and then measuring the concentrations of all three components. The hydronium ion concentration can be readily measured with a pH electrode. The others can be determined using spectroscopy if they absorb light. It is also possible to determine the K_a of a weak acid from only pH and volume measurements by constructing a **titration plot** also known as a weak acid **titration curve**.

A titration curve is a graph of pH versus volume of added **titrant**. In a weak acid titration, the titrant is a strong base, such as sodium hydroxide. Examples of two weak acid titration curves are given in Figures 10-10 and 10-11. Both involve the titration of 20 mL of a 0.100 M weak acid solution with a 0.100 M NaOH solution. The only difference is the K_a value for the weak acid used. The titration curve can allow you to calculate the concentration of the weak acid solution (moles of acid per liter of solution), and the dissociation equilibrium constant, K_a.

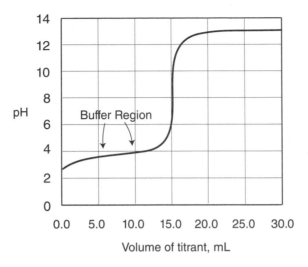

Figure 10-10. Hypothetical titration of a weak acid with a $K_a = 10^{-4}$.

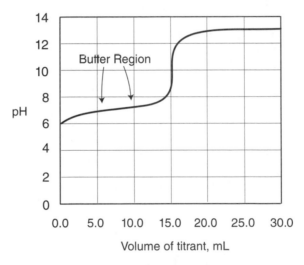

Figure 10-11. Hypothetical titration of a weak acid with a $K_a = 10^{-6}$.

At any point on these titration curves, the weak acid (HA) is in equilibrium with the hydronium ion and the conjugate base of that weak acid (A⁻). We will use the "Buffer Region" of these titration curves (the region where at least 10% of the weak acid has been titrated, but less than 90%) to help us determine values of K_a.

Performing a Weak Acid Titration

1. **Mass a sample of the weak acid.** The ideal sample size will depend on the expected molar mass of the acid and the concentration of the NaOH titrant. A sample size should be selected that will require between 25 and 50 mL of titrant. The sample mass must be measured as accurately as possible.

2. **Dissolve the acid and assemble the apparatus.** Arrange a titration setup as illustrated in Figure 10-12. Add sufficient water to dissolve the acid. Swirl gently to dissolve the acid. This is a slow process. Swirl the flasks for several seconds every minute or two until solution is complete.

3. **Preparing to titrate.** Fill the buret with a standardized solution of NaOH. Read and record the solution level in the buret. Turn on the pH meter and establish a pH reading. Record this value.

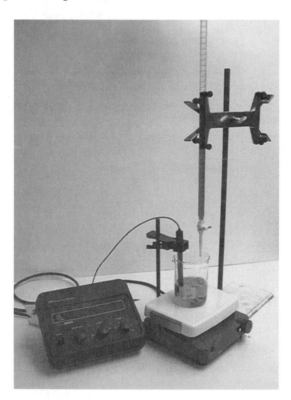

Figure 10-12. Weak acid titration setup.

4. **Titrating.** This titration is performed incrementally. A small amount of NaOH is added, equilibrium is reestablished, and the pH is measured. This is repeated as many times as necessary until the pH is distinctly basic. Before beginning the titration, examine the titration curve shown in Figure 10-13. Notice that the amount of NaOH required to produce a change in the pH differs considerably as the titration progresses. At the start, the pH changes

readily and each NaOH increment should be less than one mL. Near the half-equivalence point, the pH will not change much as more NaOH is added, so each increment can be one to two milliliters. Near the equivalence point, the pH will change drastically and the increments of NaOH will need to be very small (as small as one drop!). It is important that you add the NaOH titrant carefully throughout the titration. If you aren't careful, you may miss the equivalence point, then you will not be able to calculate the moles of weak acid in the sample.

Here are more pointers.

+ The initial pH is the pH for a titration volume of 0.

+ It should take about 30 seconds for the pH to stabilize after each addition of NaOH.

+ If you aren't careful, you can miss the equivalence point. To avoid this problem it is recommended that the volume of each increment should not exceed 2 mL, nor should any addition of NaOH produce a pH change larger than 0.2.

At the conclusion of the titration, don't forget to do the following.

+ Make sure the pH electrode is properly stored.

+ Make sure the pH meter is in proper standby mode.

+ Make sure you have securely stored your unused NaOH for the next experiment.

Evaluating a Weak Acid Titration Plot

Since pH is a measure of hydronium ion concentration and can be measured, Equation 10-5 can be rearranged to isolate this term.

$$\left[H_3O^+\right]_{eq} = K_a \frac{\left[HA\right]_{eq}}{\left[A^-\right]_{eq}}$$

(10-6)

Taking the log of both sides and multiplying by −1 gives

$$-\log\left[H_3O^+\right]_{eq} = -\log K_a + \log \frac{\left[A^-\right]_{eq}}{\left[HA\right]_{eq}}$$

(10-7)

which can be expressed in terms of pH and pK_a (where $pK_a = -\log K_a$),

$$pH = pK_a + \log \frac{\left[A^-\right]_{eq}}{\left[HA\right]_{eq}}$$

(10-8)

This equation defines the shape of the titration plot in the **buffer region**, and can be used to determine K_a.

As strong base is added and we move into the buffer region of the titration curve, the equilibrium concentration of the protonated acid ([HA]) decreases and the conjugate base concentration ([A$^-$]) increases. The first addition of base causes large changes in [A$^-$], producing large changes in the ratio and therefore large changes in pH. However, as [A$^-$] becomes larger, the relative changes in pH created by the addition of more base become smaller and smaller, eventually becoming a minimum when [HA] and [A$^-$] are equal, at the halfway point in the titration. With subsequent additions of strong base, the trend reverses. [HA] becomes smaller and smaller and the relative changes produced by base addition become larger and larger. Finally, as the end of the titration nears and [HA] becomes very small, very large changes in pH are produced.

Table 10-1. Sample data titration of a weak acid with a strong base.

Total NaOH Added (mL)	Measured pH
0.00	3.00
5.00	4.05
10.00	4.40
20.00	4.82
30.00	5.18
40.00	5.60
45.00	5.95
49.00	6.69
49.50	7.00
49.90	7.70
49.95	8.00
50.00*	8.85*
50.05	9.70
50.10	10.00
50.50	10.70
51.00	11.00
55.00	11.68
60.00	11.96
70.00	12.23

* The equivalence point

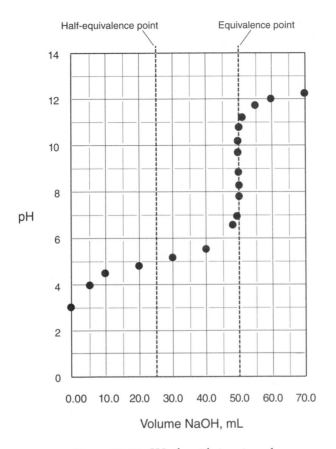

Figure 10-13. Weak acid titration plot.

A "sample" titration plot is given in Table 10-1 and graphed in Figure 10-13. Note that the number of data points taken varies as you get near the equivalence point of the titration curve, and that more points are necessary to define the rapid changes in pH which occur in this region. In our example, 2 drops of base near the equivalence point (from 49.95 mL to 50.05) causes a change in pH of 1.70 units.

Determining the Molar Mass

The total moles of HA present in the sample will be equal to the total moles of base added at the **equivalence point**. On the titration curve this is the point where the plot is going straight up and down. For the data plotted in Figure 10-13 the equivalence point is at 50.0 mL titrant. Having identified this point the moles of NaOH required can be calculated from the volume and its concentration. This will be equal to the moles of weak acid present in the sample. If the mass of acid in the sample is known then a molar mass can be calculated.

Determining the K_a

Because the equilibrium is reestablished rather rapidly after each addition of base, it is theoretically possible to calculate K_a after each addition of strong base, up to the equivalence point. The problem is accurately measuring the equilibrium concentrations of each reactant to substitute into equation 2. The $[H_3O^+]$ is not a problem as it is measured directly each time titrant is added. But the other two components, $[HA]$ and $[A^-]$, cannot be so easily determined. Fortunately, there are assumptions that can be made about $[HA]_{eq}$ and $[A^-]_{eq}$ that will allow calculation of K_a.

The most straightforward method involves the use of Equation 10-9, repeated here,

$$pH = pK_a + \log \frac{[A^-]_{eq}}{[HA]_{eq}} \qquad (10\text{-}9)$$

With this equation it is not necessary to know $[HA]_{eq}$ and $[A^-]_{eq}$ individually, but only the ratio of the moles of HA and A^- in the titration solution, in the buffer region. We can use a mass balance analysis value for this ratio. In the buffer region of the titration we can assume that,

$$\text{moles } A^-_{eq} = \text{moles } OH^-_{added} = V_b \times [NaOH] \qquad (10\text{-}10)$$

where V_b represents the volume of strong base added up to that point. We can then express the equilibrium moles of the undissociated acid, HA as

$$\text{moles } HA_{eq} = \text{moles } HA_{total} - \text{moles } A^-_{eq} = V_{b,\,equiv} \times [NaOH] - V_b \times [NaOH] \qquad (10\text{-}11)$$

We can now construct an expression for the ratio of conjugate base to weak acid in terms of titrant added:

$$\frac{[A^-]_{eq}}{[HA]_{eq}} = \frac{\left(\dfrac{\text{moles } A^-}{\text{volume of solution}}\right)_{eq}}{\left(\dfrac{\text{moles } HA}{\text{volume of solution}}\right)_{eq}} \qquad (10\text{-}12)$$

Since the volume of solution in the buffer region of the titration is the same for both A^- and HA, it can be canceled out of the equation. Continuing with our analysis, we can substitute from Equations 10-10 and 10-11 into 10-12:

$$\frac{\text{moles } A^-}{\text{moles } HA} = \frac{V_b \times C_{NaOH}}{V_{b.\,equiv} \times C_{NaOH} - V_b \times C_{NaOH}} \qquad (10\text{-}13)$$

Substituting this expression into Equation 10-8 for the ratio $[A^-]/[HA]$ yields,

$$pH = pK_a + \log\left(\frac{V_b}{V_{b.\,equiv} - V_b}\right) \qquad (10\text{-}14)$$

This equation can be used to calculate the pK_a from any point on the buffer region of the titration curve. And for one point, no calculation is required. Consider what happens when half of the titrant needed to reach the equivalence point has been added.

$$V_b = \tfrac{1}{2} V_{b,\ equiv} \tag{10-15}$$

$$pH = pK_a + \log\left(\frac{\tfrac{1}{2}V_{b.\ equiv}}{V_{b.\ equiv} - \tfrac{1}{2}V_{b.\ equiv}} \right) \tag{10-16}$$

and

$$pH = pK_a + \log(1) = pK_a \tag{10-17}$$

The volume of titrant added to reach this condition is referred to as the **half-equivalence point**. At this point the pK_a can be read directly from the titration curve (compare the two weak acids shown in Figures 10-10 and 10-11).

In practice, the best thing to do is to use all the data points in the buffer region of the titration curve to determine values for pK_a and then average them to improve the confidence level in your answer.

10-6 COMPLEXOMETRIC TITRATIONS

When in solution, metal cations, especially transition metal cations, have a tendency to form complex structures with certain molecules and multi-atomic anions called **ligands**. The reaction of metal cations with ligands to form complex ions is quite suitable to use for titrations. One very common complexing agent is ethylenediaminetetraacetic acid or EDTA. The anion, *ethylenediaminetetraacetate*, $EDTA^{-4}$, acts as a hexadentate (from the Greek meaning six-toothed) ligand and forms very stable one-to-one complexes with nearly every metal ion that can be found in solution.

$$M^{+n} + EDTA^{-4} \rightleftharpoons M - EDTA^{+(n-4)} \tag{10-18}$$

where M is any metal cation. The equilibrium expression governing this reaction is

$$K_f = \frac{\left[M - EDTA^{(+n-4)} \right]}{\left[M^{+n} \right]\left[EDTA^{-4} \right]} \tag{10-19}$$

EDTA forms such strong complexes because its three-dimensional shape creates a "cage" of the right size to accommodate most metal ions. When a metal ion enters the cage, six highly electronegative atoms are in excellent positions to form strong interactions with the metal ion.

Solution Properties

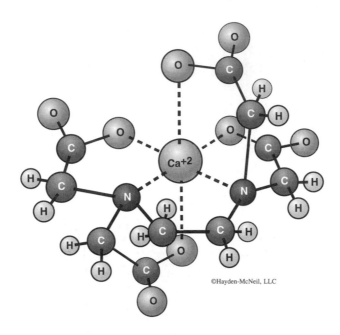

Ca^{+2} - Ethylenediaminetetraacetate complex

Figure 10-14. EDTA complex.

Two factors will affect the strength of the bond between the metal ion and the EDTA molecule. One is the charge on the ion. The more positive the charge on the ion, the stronger these interactions. The other is the size of the ion. The closer the size of the ion is to the size of the "hole" in the EDTA cage, the stronger the bond will be.

Table 10-2 lists equilibrium formation constant values for some common metal cations. The larger the value of K_f, the stronger the complex that forms will be. Note that the K_f values for +1 ions are significantly smaller than those for di- and trivalent ions. This means that EDTA can be used to distinguish between them. In an experiment using the right indicator the endpoint of the titration will be reached before the [EDTA] becomes large enough to form complexes with monovalent ions. The moles of EDTA used will be equivalent to the moles of multivalent positive ions present in the sample. (Note: with a different indicator that changes color at a higher EDTA concentration it would be possible to also titrate monovalent ions.)

Table 10-2. Formation constants for some metal–EDTA complexes.

Metal Ion	log K_f		Metal Ion	log K_f
Li^+	2.79		Mg^{+2}	8.69
Na^+	1.66		Hg^{+2}	21.7
K^+	0.8		Zn^{+2}	16.5
Ca^{+2}	10.69		Ni^{+2}	18.62
Co^{+2}	16.31		Fe^{+3}	14.33
Cu^{+2}	18.8		Al^{+3}	16.3

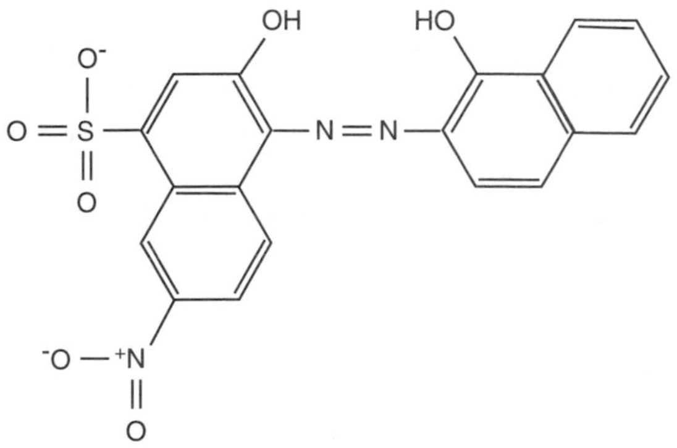

Figure 10-15. Eriochrome Black T.

Given the reaction between EDTA and divalent metal cations, it only remains to identify a method of determining when all M^{+2} has reacted to complete the setup of a titration. As with acid–base reactions, the best way is to find a suitable indicator. In the case of divalent metal cations, an indicator is a molecule which forms a complex having a different color than the free ion. Such a molecule is an organic dye called Eriochrome Black T (Erio-T).

This dye itself is a triprotic acid and is often abbreviated H_3In. However, the sulfonic acid group is such a strong acid it is always ionized in solution.

The degree of ionization of the other two protons will depend on the pH.

The color of the free dye is dependent on its state of ionization.

$$H_2In^- \quad \rightleftharpoons \quad HIn^{-2} \quad \rightleftharpoons \quad In^{-3} \tag{10-20}$$

(red)   pH 9   (blue)   pH 11   (yellow)

Regardless of the degree of ionization, when it is complexed with magnesium, it is red. The color change observed when the metal-indicator complex dissociates depends on the pH.

at pH = 7

$$H_2In^- + Mg^{+2} + 2\,H_2O \quad \rightleftharpoons \quad MgIn^- + 2\,H_3O^+ \qquad (10\text{-}21)$$
(red) (red)

at pH = 10

$$HIn^{-2} + Mg^{+2} + H_2O \quad \rightleftharpoons \quad MgIn^- + H_3O^+ \qquad (10\text{-}22)$$
(blue) (red)

Erio-T forms complexes only with magnesium. This raises the question of how it can be used as an indicator for a titration to determine total multivalent metal cation concentration. The answer is twofold. First, take a look at the K_f values for the EDTA complexes (Table 10-2). Note that the value for the magnesium complex is the smallest of all the multivalent ions. This means that as EDTA is added to a sample, the magnesium complex will not form until all other divalent metal ions have been complexed.

The other consideration is that samples to be titrated must contain enough magnesium to form the MgIn-complex. Most groundwater sources that have not been purified contain sufficient Mg^{+2} to allow use of Erio-T. For samples with no detectable Mg^{+2} either another indicator needs to be selected, or some Mg^{+2} needs to be added.

The chemistry of the titration is as follows. When Erio-T is added to a solution containing Mg^{+2}, the complex forms and the solution turns red. Next EDTA is added from a buret. As the EDTA is added, it will form a complex with the metal cation having the LARGEST formation constant (K_f). Once that cation is complexed, any more EDTA added will form a complex with the cation having the next largest formation constant. This will continue, with no apparent change in the solution (no color change) until the EDTA begins complexing the Mg^{+2} present in the sample. As the EDTA complexes with the Mg^{+2}, the free magnesium ion concentration ($[Mg^{+2}]$) will become so small that the reaction of equation 10-22 will proceed to the left to reestablish equilibrium and the magnesium-indicator complex will dissociate. If the pH is between 9 and 11 the solution will turn from red to blue indicating the endpoint of the titration. Since both complexes are strong, this change should occur with less than one drop of EDTA titrant producing a very sharp endpoint.

Control of the pH is crucial in this titration. If the solution is too acidic, the free indicator (H_2In^-) is the same color as the complex (see Equation 10-21). If the pH drops much below 9, no endpoint will be observed. The best results are obtained if the pH is maintained at a value of 10. During the course of the titration two moles of hydronium ion will be released by every mole of EDTA titrant added. Thus sufficient pH 10 buffer must be added to neutralize this added acid and keep the pH from dropping.

Performing a Complexometric Titration

This titration is performed like a simple acid/base titration with one exception. To ensure that the reactions all occur correctly a pH buffer must be added. The amount of buffer required will depend on the amount of EDTA to be added. 10 mL will suffice for most normal water samples, but may not be enough for highly concentrated samples. If you have trouble with the endpoint, try using more buffer.

Titrations should be performed until reproducible results are obtained. In general, three trials that agree (within the limits of accuracy of the technique) are considered the minimum necessary to demonstrate reproducibility. If the titration volumes are not ideal (between 10 and 50 mL) you should consider changing the sample volume or making a new EDTA solution.

1. **The titrant.** The EDTA titrant is provided as the disodium salt, $Na_2H_2C_{10}H_{12}N_2O_8$ (abbreviated as Na_2H_2EDTA). Determining how to make up your titrant solution is left to you. This solid material is very stable and can be accurately weighed to make a solution of known concentration with an accuracy of at least three significant figures. Standardization is not required. You will need to decide what concentration to make and how much to make. See chapter 11 for guidance. To avoid problems with the titration, the concentration of EDTA you prepare should be no less than 0.001 M and no more than 0.1 M.

2. **General preparation.** Clean all the glassware you intend to use. Not only should your glassware be clean, but you must also guard against dilution error by making sure you rinse glassware with the appropriate solutions before filling.

3. **Indicator preparation.** The preferred indicator is an organic dye called Eriochrome Black T, or Erio-T for short. It is provided as a solid. Obtain a small amount of this indicator in a small beaker or on a watch glass. Since it is tough to add the same amount to each titration sample it is suggested that you make up a solution of the indicator to use for the day. This is easily done by putting a small amount of the indicator in a small beaker and adding distilled water to produce a very dark solution. This solution can then be added to titration flasks using a transfer pipet. Note that the indicator is unstable in solution and will go bad after a few hours.

4. **Titrating.** Prepare a titration flask containing your sample, 10 mL of buffer, and sufficient indicator to provide a noticeable color. Fill the buret with your EDTA titrant solution. Record the volume. Place the flask underneath the buret tip. Begin adding the titrant. Swirl the flask and watch the color. At

some point the color will begin to change. Slow down the addition and continue to swirl. When the color is completely blue stop adding titrant. Continue swirling. The color should fade back to red. Add more titrant until the color returns to blue. Again, swirl and watch to see if it fades back. Continue this process until the color remains blue. This is the endpoint of the titration.

10-7 SPECTROPHOTOMETRIC CONCENTRATION DETERMINATION

Yet one more method to determine the concentration of things in solution is absorption spectroscopy. The amount of light absorbed by a solution is directly proportional to the number of atoms or molecules doing the absorbing, making spectroscopy a valuable tool. It is by far the quickest, easiest, and cheapest method available for the direct determination of numbers of atoms and molecules. As a result, it is widely employed in labs in many disciplines.

The Beer-Lambert Law

The relationship between absorbance and concentration is known as the **Beer-Lambert law**, or more commonly, Beer's law,

$$A = \varepsilon bc \tag{10-23}$$

where "A" is the measured absorbance, "c," the concentration of the absorbing species, "b," the path length of the sample (width of the cuvet) and "ε" a proportionality constant known as the **molar absorptivity** (which has units of $M^{-1}cm^{-1}$). The molar absorptivity is constant for a specific chemical compound and a specific wavelength.

For every compound there is typically at least one wavelength in which ε reaches a maximum. This wavelength is known as the λ_{max} and is normally chosen to carry out absorption spectroscopy of that compound. For example, consider the visible spectrum of hemoglobin (Figure 10-16). There are three λ_{max} values in the visible range that would be suitable: 412, 541, and 576 nm.

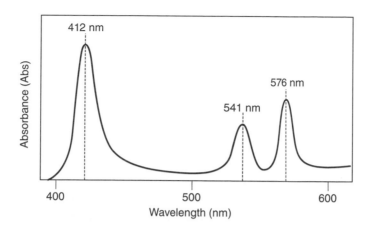

Figure 10-16. Absorption spectrum of hemoglobin.

If the molar absorptivity is known at a particular wavelength, the concentration of a chemical compound present in a transparent sample can be calculated from the measured absorbance using Beer's law. The simplest way to determine ε is to take a solution of known concentration, select the wavelength for which the value of ε is desired (usually the wavelength where the absorbance has its greatest value), measure the absorbance there, and measure the path length. The above equation can be rearranged to solve for ε and the value computed from the experimental measurements. The result, however, may not be reliable. For example, our spectrophotometers produce reliable results only in the absorbance range of 0.01 to 1.0. A value outside this range will have questionable meaning. It is also possible for other effects to cause the behavior of the solution not to follow the Beer-Lambert law.

A more accurate method to determine ε is to measure the absorbance of a number of solutions of different concentrations and construct a **calibration plot**. Beer's law is a linear equation of the form $y = mx + b$ (b, the y intercept, is zero and therefore does not appear in the Beer's law equation).

$$A = \varepsilon b \ \ c$$
$$\downarrow \quad \downarrow \ \downarrow$$
$$y = m \ \ x$$

A plot of absorbance vs. concentration should produce a straight line with a slope equal to εb. Figure 10-17 is a representation of such a plot.

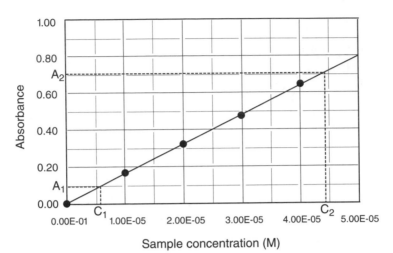

Figure 10-17. Beer's law plot of absorbance data.

Determining a Molar Absorptivity

If the molar absorptivity of a compound is known, then determining the compound's concentration in solution is simple. Measure the absorptivity and use the Beer-Lambert equation (10-23) to calculate the concentration. Unfortunately, the molar absorptivity is frequently unknown. The following is a description of how to determine a molar absorptivity given a pure sample of the compound.

1. Cuvets

The determination is best performed with two cuvets. One is for the reference solution, the other for your samples. The reference cuvet is a clean, plastic cuvet filled 3/4 full with distilled water. For the sample cuvet, you will need to determine the path length for your Beer's Law analysis. The best way to measure the path length is with a Vernier caliper. If one is not available, a ruler will have to suffice.

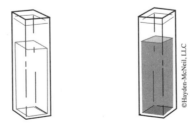

Figure 10-18. Reference and sample cuvets.

2. Standards

Remember that to determine the molar absorptivity you will need to construct a plot like the one show in Figure 10-17. This in turn requires solutions of known concentration of the compound. A series of solution can be constructed from a stock solution by performing either a serial or a parallel dilution. These are described in Chapter 11. If the pure compound is a solid, a stock solution will have to be made first. This is also discussed in Chapter 11.

The number and concentrations of solutions to be made is dependent on the particular experiment begin performed. Since you only need enough of each solution to make an absorbance measurement, 10 mL will normally be plenty. 6 inch test tubes are very convenient for making and holding these solutions.

3. Measurements

Given a pair of cuvets and a series of standards here are the steps necessary to collect the data required to construct a plot like the one shown in Figure 10-17.

+ Prepare the spectrophotometer for absorbance measurements as described in Chapter 8.

+ Rinse and then fill the sample cuvet with the most concentrated standard solution. Put it in the cell holder and start collecting.

+ Identify the wavelength of maximal absorbance (λ_{max}). Use the cursor to determine the wavelength. Don't forget to record this value in your notebook. You may also want to save the spectrum data file.

+ Read and record the absorbance. Begin your working plot in your notebook.

+ Remove the sample cuvet and empty it. Identify the most *dilute* solution. Rinse the cuvet with a small amount and then fill the cuvet. Put it in the cell holder. Read and record the absorbance at λ_{max}.

+ Repeat the last step with the remaining solutions, working your way from the least concentrated to the most concentrated.

NOTES

1. If the absorbance of your sample solution is greater than 1.0, it is too concentrated. You will need to dilute it.
2. To avoid dilution error, make sure you rinse the cuvet with some of the solution before filling it. Cuvets should be filled to between 2/3 and 3/4.
3. If your measurements do not produce a linear plot, then the Beer's Law analysis will not be valid. As you make your measurements continue to plot them and check to see if they fit a linear plot. Any deviations from linearity should be questioned and addressed while you are still in lab.

4. Analysis

Determining ε requires determining the slope of the best-fit line through the data points. The first step is to determine which data points are credible. Any that are questionable should be discarded. Note that because the intercept in the Beer's law equation is zero, a concentration value of zero should produce a zero absorbance and the origin of the plot (0,0) should be a point on the plot. However, due to other effects this may not be true for any particular analysis. It may be necessary to discard the 0,0 data point.

If you construct your plot in Excel, the slope can be obtained by adding a trend line to the plot. This is discussed in Chapter 2. Assuming you have plotted your data so that the absorbance values are y and the concentrations are x then the slope displayed by Excel will be equal to εb, the molar absorptivity times the cuvet path length (measured in cm).

Alternately, the slope can be determined directly from a data plot. Consider the data graphed in Figure 10-17. By selecting two points on the line and reading their coordinates, the slope can be calculated. To avoid biasing the readings, the points selected for this determination should not be the same as any of the data points.

$$\varepsilon b = \text{slope} = \frac{A_2 - A_1}{C_2 - C_1} = \frac{0.70 - 0.10}{4.4 \times 10^{-5}\,M - 0.60 \times 10^{-5}\,M} = 1.6 \times 10^4\,M^{-1} \quad (10\text{-}24)$$

It is also possible to read the concentration of an unknown sample directly from a calibration plot by **interpolation** using the measured absorbance of the unknown sample. In the example shown in Figure 10-19, an absorbance reading of 0.45 produces a concentration of $2.8 \times 10{-}5$ M.

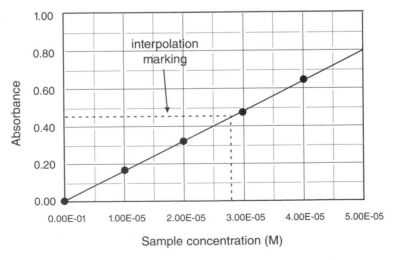

Figure 10-19. Interpolating concentrations from a Beer's law plot.

11

SOLUTION PREPARATION

Making solutions is a basic skill required of anyone working in a chemical lab. This chapter presents some of the more important hows and whys of solution making.

+ Concentration.

+ Making solutions from solids.

+ Dilutions.

The solutions required to perform chemical experiments can all be placed in one of three categories, each with its own distinctive terminology.

+ **Reagents** are chemicals required to perform an experiment. This will include the chemicals required for a chemical reaction to occur and those required to maintain constant reaction conditions.

+ **Standards** (*also referred to as "knowns"*) are required to confirm results or to provide the information needed to calibrate the instrument or technique. Standards are made from pure chemicals of known composition.

+ **Samples** are the objects of qualitative and quantitative analyses. Solid samples are often made into solutions for ease of analysis. For example, a spectrophotometer will accommodate solutions, but not solids.

While chemical investigations are sometimes done in the gas phase or the solid phase, most are done in solution. The main advantages to experimentation with solutions are the speed at which the reactions occur, the ease of measurements, and the ability to precisely control and monitor reaction conditions.

Preparing solutions can be viewed as two separate operations—deciding what to make, then making it. Each operation involves collecting information and making a number of decisions. The following is a detailed discussion of the process.

11-1 CONCENTRATION

In order to make solutions one must understand the various terms used and the idea of *concentration*. In chemistry, concentration refers to the amount of *solute* present in a solution. The solute is what is dissolved in the *solvent* to make the solution. The concentration of the solution is an intensive property and is used to determine how much of a solution to use to deliver a given amount of solute.

Concentration is a ratio of amounts. Normally these are expressed as mass, volume or amounts of matter (moles). By far, the most common units of concentration are *percent composition* and *molarity*.

Percent Composition

When the chemical composition of the sample is not known, concentrations are often expressed as percentages. The most common is a weight-to-volume ratio—the ratio of the sample weight, in grams, to the total volume of solution in mL. Thus, a "2% water solution" describes 2 grams of a solid sample dissolved in enough water to make 100 mL of solution. Note that the ratio compares grams to milliliters.

A weight-to-volume ratio is not the only way percent composition can be expressed. Weight-to-weight and volume-to-volume are also possible. To avoid confusion, the type of ratio is often indicated using an abbreviation: (w/v) indicates a weight-to-volume ratio (weight of solute to volume of solutions). A 50% (v/v) solution of glycerin in water indicates a solution made from 50 mL of glycerine diluted to 100 mL with water. If no designation is made, you are to assume a weight-to-volume ratio.

Molarity

Molarity is the number of moles of solute present in one liter of the solution. It is the preferred unit of concentration in chemistry because chemical reactions are written in terms of moles. Making molar solutions requires some way to measure out moles of chemicals. For a dilution the moles of chemical can be determined from the molarity of the original solution and the volume used. For a solid chemical the moles can be determined from the mass of the chemical and its molar mass.

11-2 DECIDING WHAT TO MAKE

The first operation is to define the solution to be made. With reagents this can be quite easy. Many techniques specify exactly the reagents required. Other times, some decisions will need to be made. These could be such things as the solution concentration, the characteristics of the solvent (polarity, pH, redox potential, etc.), and the characteristics of any spectator ions. For example, the concentration of a titrant should be selected to provide a convenient titration volume. The concentration of a buffer will need to be high enough to "soak up" all added acid or base. An acid used to change the pH must be one whose anion does not cause other problems.

In addition to the above considerations, defining standard solutions also requires knowledge of the expected experimental results. For a quantitative determination, standards should be selected that cover the range of possible results. For a qualitative analysis, standards must provide a representative sampling of possible outcomes.

Defining sample solutions can be even trickier. Such issues as solubility, pH, reactivity, and concentration must be considered. For example, samples can be too dark to measure reliably in a spectrometer. A sample may not be soluble in water at the pH required by a test. Complex samples (e.g., dirt) require consideration of the sampling procedure.

The following is a suggested approach to designing a solution:

1. Create a list of the characteristics it must have. What must it do and what characteristics must it have to be reliable?

2. Determine the composition of the solution that will produce the desired characteristics. What goes into it? Include things like chemical species, solvents, and pH buffers and adjustors.

3. Determine the concentration of species which will produce the desired characteristics. For a procedure based on a chemical reaction this will usually be molarity (M).

11-3 MAKING SOLUTIONS FROM SOLIDS

The second operation is to create the designed solution. This requires making decisions and performing operations. Sometimes these are constrained by the experiment being performed. They may also be constrained by the nature and amount of your sample. The following is a summary:

- **Select a container.** First the total volume of solution required is determined, then an appropriate container is selected. A beaker will work for a solution requiring only one significant figure accuracy. A graduated cylinder is good if two to three significant figures are needed. An even more accurate device is a *volumetric flask*. When filled to the mark, a volumetric flask contains its design volume to four or five significant figures. (Note: a volumetric flask **contains** an exact volume. It will not **deliver** an exact volume because some of the measured volume will cling to the walls of the flask.)

- **Choose the chemical(s)** to add to produce the desired outcome. Usually, only one chemical is required, but sometimes two or more are needed to produce the desired effect. An example of the latter is the preparation of a buffer having a specific pH. This will require both a weak acid and its conjugate base. Determining the amounts of each to use requires the weak acid constant (K_a) and the corresponding equation.

- **Determine how much** of the chemical to obtain. A unit-analysis approach is best. Write down the quantity you want to make. Multiply by the appropriate amounts and/or conversion factors to cancel unwanted units. Continue until only measurable amounts remain. A percent solution is the simplest example.

Figuring a Percent Composition Solution

To prepare a percent composition solution, first determine if you are making a weight-to-weight, weight-to-volume, or volume-to-volume solution. Then you can compute the mass of solute to be dissolved and the amount of solution to be prepared.

Percent Composition Example: Make 250 mL of a 2.0% (w/v) sugar solution.

$$\% \text{ composition} = \frac{\text{grams chemical species}}{\text{total solution volume in mL}}$$

$$\frac{2.0 \text{ g sugar}}{100 \text{ mL solution}} \times \frac{250 \text{ mL solution}}{1} = 5.0 \text{ g sugar}$$

Because the concentration is to only two significant figures, this solution could be prepared in a graduated cylinder. Select a 250 mL (or larger) cylinder, weigh five grams of the sugar, add it to the cylinder. Add water to the 250 mL mark and mix.

Figuring a Molar Solution

$$\text{Molarity (M)} = \frac{\text{moles solute (mol)}}{\text{liters of solution (L)}} \tag{11-1}$$

$$\text{molar mass (MM)} = \frac{\text{grams (g)}}{\text{mole (mol)}} \tag{11-2}$$

To make a molar solution starting with solid solute

1. determine the number of moles of chemical (solute) required from the volume and molarity of the desired solution, and then

2. use the moles of solute and its molar mass to determine the mass in grams of solute to weigh out.

> **Molar Example:** Make 150 mL of a 0.150 M sodium nitrate solution. A jar of solid sodium nitrate ($NaNO_3$) is available.
>
> 1. Molarity $NaNO_3 \times$ volume of solution = moles of $NaNO_3$ required
>
> $$\frac{0.150 \text{ mole } NaNO_3}{1 \text{ L solution}} \times \frac{0.250 \text{ L solution}}{1} = 0.0375 \text{ mole of } NaNO_3$$
>
> 2. Moles of $NaNO_3 \times$ molar mass $NaNO_3$ = grams of $NaNO_3$ required
>
> $$\frac{0.0375 \text{ mole } NaNO_3}{1} \times \frac{85.00 \text{ g } NaNO_3}{\text{mole } NaNO_3} = 3.19 \text{ g } NaNO_3$$

Mixing Solutions

To ensure a uniform distribution of chemicals, solutions must be mixed. Here are two techniques commonly employed.

+ **Using a stir rod.** A stir rod is an inert object used to mix a solution. Glass is the best material to use for a stir rod, as it is least likely to chemically react with the solution. (Metal stir rods react with lots of chemicals, acids in particular.) To avoid contamination of your solution, the stir rod must be clean and must never be placed directly on the lab bench. A medium-sized beaker makes a convenient support for a stir rod.

©Hayden-McNeil, LLC

Figure 11-1. Using a stir rod.

+ **Using a magnetic stir plate.** A stir plate consists of an electric motor with a magnet attached to the top of the motor shaft. When the motor turns, the magnet spins. The motor and magnet are covered with a chemically inert cover plate. To use a stir plate, a clean magnetic stir bar (teflon-coated magnet) is placed in the solution to be mixed. The container is placed on the stir plate and moved around until the magnets line up. The stir plate motor is turned on and the speed adjusted until the stir bar is spinning smoothly and the vortex over the stir bar is not very deep.

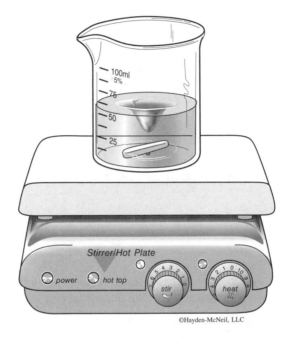

Figure 11-2. Using a stir plate.

Summary of Steps in Making a Solution

+ Select a container.

+ Choose the chemical(s).

+ Determine how much chemical(s) to use.

+ Obtain the chemical.

+ Dissolve the chemical in solvent.

+ Mix.

11-4 DILUTIONS

One rather quick way to make a solution of known concentration is by exact dilution from a more concentrated solution of known concentration. This technique is commonly used when a series of solutions of different concentrations are needed. There are two approaches to consider.

Figuring a Dilution

1. Determine the required **number of moles** of chemical from the volume and the molarity of the desired solution.

2. Determine the required **volume** of the stock reagent by dividing the required number of moles by the stock solution's concentration.

Dilution Example: Make 50.00 mL of a 3.00×10^{-2} M $CaCl_2$ solution. A stock solution of 0.200 M $CaCl_2$ is available.

---

1. M dilute $CaCl_2 \times$ Volume of dilute $CaCl_2$ = moles of $CaCl_2$ required

$$\frac{0.0300 \text{ mole } CaCl_2}{1 \text{ L solution}} \times \frac{0.05000 \text{ L solution}}{1} = 0.00150 \text{ mole } CaCl_2$$

2. moles of $CaCl_2$ needed $\times \dfrac{1}{\text{M stock } CaCl_2}$ = volume of stock $CaCl_2$ solution

$$0.00150 \text{ mole } CaCl_2 \times \frac{1 \text{ L stock solution}}{0.200 \text{ mole } CaCl_2} = 0.00750 \text{ L}$$

---

3. **Performing the dilution.** The calculated volume for the stock solution is measured and put into an appropriate container. Solvent is then added. Usually this is distilled water. It is important to remember that solution volumes are not additive. Mixing 10.00 mL of a stock solution and 90.00 mL of solvent may produce slightly less than or even more than 100.00 mL of solution. The actual amount of solvent needed is not easy to determine. Instead, solvent is usually added until the correct volume is obtained.

A Serial Dilution

A series of solutions where each solution made becomes the source solution for the next solution in the series. The advantage is that a broad range of concentrations can be had with this approach. The disadvantage is that any measurement errors made early on will be propagated through the remaining solutions. Here is how to perform a serial 1:10 dilution of a standard solution. Figure 11-3 is a schematic representation.

+ Rinse a 10 mL volumetric pipet with some of the stock solution and pipet 10.00 mL into a clean 100 mL volumetric flask. Add distilled water to the mark and then thoroughly mix. You have just prepared a solution that is exactly **one-tenth** the concentration of the stock solution.

+ Repeat the above process using the new solution in place of the stock solution. This will produce a third solution exactly one-tenth as concentrated as the second.

+ This process is repeated as many times as needed.

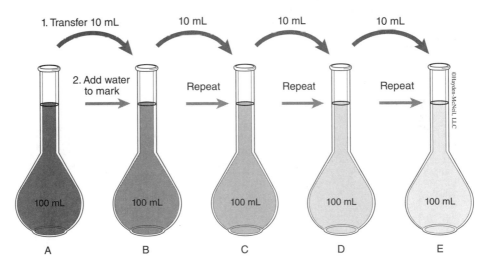

[E] = 1/10 [D] = 1/10 [C] = 1/10 [B] = 1/10 [A]

Figure 11-3. Serial dilution.

A Parallel Dilution

A series of solutions where all are made from the same original solution. Errors are less critical, but the range of solutions that can be made is more limited. Figure 11-4 is a schematic representation.

+ Rinse a 10 mL graduated pipet with some of the stock solution. Pipet 1.00 mL into a clean 100 mL volumetric flask. Add distilled water to the mark and then thoroughly mix. You have just prepared a solution which is exactly **one-hundredth** the concentration of the stock solution.

+ Using the same graduated pipet, put 2.00 mL into a clean 100 mL volumetric flask. Add distilled water to the mark and then thoroughly mix. You have just prepared a solution which is exactly **two-hundredths** the concentration of the stock solution.

+ This process is repeated as many times as needed.

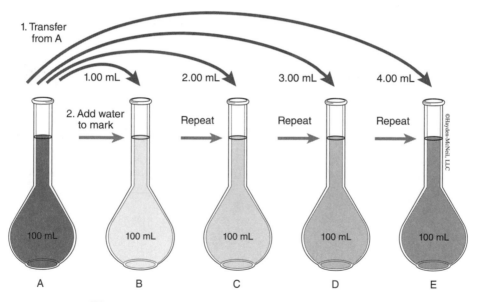

[B] = 1/100 [A] ; [C] = 2/100 [A] ; [D] = 3/100 [A] ; [E]= 4/100 [A]

Figure 11-4. Parallel dilution.

12

CHEMICAL SYNTHESIS

One of the more important functions of chemistry is the **synthesis** of useful molecules. This chapter discusses the various decisions required to carry out a successful chemical synthesis.

+ Performing the reaction.

+ Reflux.

+ Extracting and drying liquid products.

In the last century and a half, the number of compounds that can be made by chemical synthesis has mushroomed. Thousands of laboratories in industry and academia the world over are responsible for the discoveries that have led to the vast array of materials available in our world today. Perhaps the most important application of synthetic organic chemistry is the manufacture of medications. Pharmaceutical companies employ large numbers of organic chemists to develop new drugs and to seek out better ways to make existing drugs.

Chemical syntheses can be broken down into three basic processes: you make it, you isolate it, and you characterize it.

Making chemicals is the actual synthesis. It involves performing chemical reactions under conditions that maximize the quantity and purity of the desired chemical. Techniques for controlling reactions to obtain a desired outcome are described in this chapter.

Isolating the products requires the separation of the desired chemical from all the other components of the reaction mixture. The most commonly used techniques are discussed in Chapters 7 and 8.

Characterization is the process of confirming that the isolated chemical is actually the desired chemical and determining how much was made. Melting point and boiling point determinations (Chapter 7) can be used to identify the product. Chromatography (Chapter 6) can be used to determine the purity of the product. And percent yield (Chapter 2) is commonly used to help describe the success of the synthesis.

12-1 PERFORMING A SYNTHESIS

What to Include

The chemical equation will define what must be included. In general you will need the reactant materials and a solvent in which to dissolve the reactants. The solvent is needed so that the reactants will be able to come in contact with each other and react. If one of the reactants is a liquid it might be possible for it to function as the solvent as well. Other possible components are catalysts and an acid or a base to control the pH.

Amounts of Materials

The chemical equation will also be your guide to the amounts of materials to use. From the amount of product you wish to make you can back calculate how much of the reactants to use. Most often one of the reactants is added in excess. In this case the reactant that is not in excess is known as the **limiting reagent**. It is used when calculating a **percent yield** to determine the success of the reaction. Percent yields are discussed in chapter 2.

The amount of solvent will need to be sufficient to dissolve the reactants.

The order of addition of reactants and solvent is often important. Usually one or more of the reactants needs to be dissolved in the solvent before initiating the reaction. If a catalyst is used it is often what is added to initiate the reaction.

Containing the Reaction

Two factors must be considered when selecting a container for the reaction—will the reaction need to be heated or cooled and is the reaction sensitive to water or air?

If the reaction needs to be cooled an ice bath will probably be employed. The container will need to be convenient for putting in an ice bath. A beaker may suffice but an Erlenmeyer flask may be a better choice. It is easier to clamp the neck of the flask to hold it upright than to secure a beaker. For some applications, it might be useful to add rock salt to the ice to lower the temperature.

Heating the Reaction

There are three common methods of heating reactions. The simplest is to put the container directly on a hot plate. But it is difficult to control the temperature and may result in overheating the reaction. A better approach is to use a hot water bath. Figure 12-1 illustrates the use of a hot water bath.

The third is to use a heating mantle—a hot device designed to fit snuggly around a round-bottom flask. Figure 12-4 includes such a device. The heating mantle is connected to a power supply which is used to control the heat.

One major concern with the heating of a reaction mixture is the loss of solvent. This is normally addressed using the process known as **reflux** which is described in the next section.

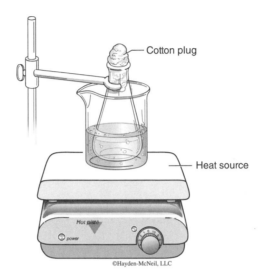

Figure 12-1. Heating a reaction.

Excluding Water and/or Air

Some reactions are sensitive to water vapor, oxygen, or other things in the air. These chemicals can cause side reactions to occur or even stop the desired reaction. For such reactions it is necessary to prevent water vapor or air from entering the reaction chamber. Water vapor can be excluded in a couple of ways. Figure 12-1 shows the use of a cotton plug. For more sensitive reactions a drying tube is employed. Figure 12-2 illustrates a drying tube. The tube is filled with a material that absorbs water. The tube is sealed to the reaction vessel so that any air entering the vessel must pass through the drying material.

Excluding oxygen in the air is more difficult. This is usually achieved by passing an inert gas over the surface of the reaction mixture.

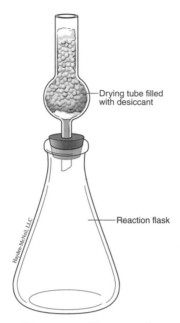

Figure 12-2. Drying tube.

Controlling fumes

Some reactions generate noxious fumes that should not be released into the room air. The primary method of controlling fumes is by performing the reaction in a fume hood. But for small containers generating a limited amount of fumes a mini-hood can be constructed on a lab bench. Figure 12-3 illustrates such a device. It consists of a funnel connected to a vacuum outlet with a short piece of rubber tubing.

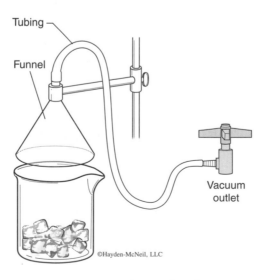

Figure 12-3. A mini hood.

Timing the Reaction

Reactions take time to occur. Sometimes measuring the time is important and other times not. If the time is important then the "start" and "end" of the reaction need to be identified and noted in the lab notebook. The start of the reaction is usually denoted by the addition of a critical component. For example, if the reaction requires a catalyst then the reaction can be "started" by adding the catalyst to the assembled components. Likewise, stopping a reaction can be achieved by removing or destroying one of the reactants. For example, if one of the reactants is destroyed by water the reaction can be stopped by adding water.

Summary of Steps

+ Determine amounts of reactants and solvent to use. Determine the order in which reactants and solvent need to be added.

+ Determine whether heating or cooling is required and whether the reaction needs to be isolated from the atmosphere.

+ Select an appropriate container for the reaction. If a reflux is required, set up the appropriate equipment.

+ Set up the reaction vessel and mix the reactants, solvent, catalyst (if any), and any other required materials in the right order.

+ Stop the reaction at the appropriate time.

+ Proceed to perform the appropriate isolation and characterization procedures.

12-2 REFLUX

Consider a reaction where the reactants are dissolved in a solvent and the reaction mixture needs to be heated. Over the course of the reaction, solvent will be lost due to evaporation. It is also quite possible that reactants will also be lost due to evaporation. The loss of solvent and reactants could change the outcome of the reaction. The evaporated solvent is also an undesired contamination of the environment. When heating a solvent mixture it is necessary to avoid solvent (and reactant) loss. This is most commonly done using a **reflux apparatus**.

Figure 12-4. Reflux apparatus.

Reflux is the process of causing the solvent to condense and fall back into the reaction vessel. This is achieved by placing a cold jacket around the outlet of the reaction vessel. As solvent vapors rise out of the reaction vessel they encounter the cold jacket, condense back into the liquid state and drop back into the reaction flask. For this reason the cold jacket is known as a "**condenser.**"

Figure 12-4 illustrates a reflux setup. The heating mantle heats the round-bottom reaction flask. Hot solvent rises up into the condenser where it is condensed back to the liquid state. A steady flow of cold water through the condenser jacket keeps the temperature of the condenser walls below the condensation point of the solvent. The water flow and heat applied by the heating mantle must be adjusted to produce the best balance. A good balance has been achieved when a ring of condensed solvent can be observed low down in the condenser.

12-3 EXTRACTING AND DRYING LIQUID PRODUCTS

Consider a reaction where the product is a liquid. It may contain dissolved impurities. One way to remove those impurities is by extraction. In this technique the impurity is caused to move from the liquid product into another solvent that does not mix with the product. The most common application is using water to remove water-soluble materials from a water-insoluble liquid product. The following is an outline of a procedure for doing so.

- Place the material in a centrifuge tube. Slowly, while shaking, add the extracting solvent until the volumes of the two layers are about equal.

- Allow the two layers to separate. Centrifugation may help if the layers do not readily separate.

- Once the layers have separated remove the extracting solvent using a transfer pipet and place it in another container.

- Repeat the extraction at least once and more times as needed.

- Finally, it may be necessary to dry the product. This is done by adding a small amount of a drying agent to the product while still in the centrifuge tube. Shake and allow the solid to settle to the bottom of the tube. The product can then be removed using a transfer pipet. Common drying agents are anhydrous sodium sulfate and anhydrous magnesium sulfate.

INDEX